CW00925472

THE ECCENTRIC BILLIONAIRE

THE
ECCENTRIC BILLIONAIRE

JOHN D. MACARTHUR—
EMPIRE BUILDER, RELUCTANT PHILANTHROPIST,
RELENTLESS ADVERSARY

NANCY KRIPLEN

AMERICAN MANAGEMENT ASSOCIATION

New York • Atlanta • Brussels • Chicago • Mexico City • San Francisco
Shanghai • Tokyo • Toronto • Washington, D.C.

This publication is designed to provide accurate and authoritative information in regard to the subject matter covered. It is sold with the understanding that the publisher is not engaged in rendering legal, accounting, or other professional service. If legal advice or other expert assistance is required, the services of a competent professional person should be sought.

Library of Congress Cataloging-in-Publication Data

Kriplen, Nancy.
   The eccentric billionaire : John D. MacArthur—empire builder, reluctant philanthropist, relentless adversary / Nancy Kriplen.
       p. cm.
   Includes bibliographical references and index.
   ISBN-13: 978-0-8144-0889-6
   ISBN-10: 0-8144-0889-3
   1. MacArthur, John D., 1897–1978. 2. Capitalists and financiers—United States—Biography. 3. Billionaires—United States—Biography. 4. Businesspeople—United States—Biography. 5. Philanthropists—United States—Biography. I. Title. II. Title: John D. MacArthur—empire builder, reluctant philanthropist, relentless adversary.
HG172.M28K75 2008
368.0092—dc22
[B]
2007031227

Printing number
10 9 8 7 6 5 4 3 2 1

To Dave, always,
and
Marsh, Kate, Madelyn

CONTENTS

viii   Contents

ACKNOWLEDGMENTS

Roaring through the inky darkness, sports car drivers and navigators competing in twenty-four-hour road rallies such as the Michigan Milia are likely to talk the night away in an effort to stay awake. It was on such occasions that my future husband heard tales from his pal Sandy MacArthur about Sandy's colorful and eccentric "Uncle John." What a great subject for a biography, I thought, as I, too, later heard these stories from Sandy.

By the time I was ready to attempt to capture this life on paper, a remarkable project had already been completed that aided my work immensely. In the 1980s the John D. and Catherine T. MacArthur Foundation funded the research and writing of a slim book about the MacArthur family origins, which was given private and limited distribution. *The MacArthur Heritage: The Story of an American Family* was written by the historian Barbara Graymont, based on John Taylor's extensive interviews, primarily with those who knew John MacArthur's family in its early days.

Both Dr. Graymont and Dr. Taylor were faculty members at Nyack College, a religious school with MacArthur family connections. Dr. Graymont, former dean of the school's history department, is an experienced and graceful writer of history, and Dr. Taylor, a cheerful, indefatigable interviewer. These interviews have been particularly valuable, since many of those whom he interviewed are no longer living.

And so my thanks to the scholarship of Barbara Graymont and John Taylor, and to the late Sandy MacArthur and his wife Billie, and, of course, to my husband, Dave, for introducing me to this fascinating family in the first place. All have provided a platform on which I could continue the story of John D. MacArthur.

I am grateful to the following institutions, organizations, libraries, and archives, and to their knowledgeable staff members, past and present: American Legion National Headquarters Library (Kevin Flanagan); American Museum of Natural History (Barbara Mathé); Asolo Theatre (Vic Meyrich); *Atlanta Journal–Constitution* (Janine Williams); Atlanta-Fulton Public Library (Richard Cruse, Shirley Thomas); AXA Equitable Archives (Jonathan Coss); Bankers Life and Casualty Co. (Kert Brown, Barbara Ciesemeier, Milan Huba, Katherine Kaluso, Erwin McKendry, Janice Marszalek); Canadian Genealogy Centre, Library and Archives Canada (Mary Munk, Lorraine St. Louis-Harrison); Center on Philanthropy at Indiana University (William Enright); Chicago History Museum (Rob Medina, Debbie Vaughan); Chicago Public Library; Cleveland Public Library–Business, Economics and Labor Department.

Thanks also to: Federal Trade Commission (Richard Stevens); The Feil Organization (Marty Bernstein, Jeffrey Feil); Florida State Library and Archives (Crista M. Hosmer); Florida State University (Laraine Correll, Richard G. Fallon, Mary Gunderlach, Lynn Hogan); Frank Lloyd Wright Preservation Trust, Research Center (Valerie Harris); Gerald R. Ford Presidential Library (Joshua Cochran); Historical Museum of South Florida (Dawn R. Hugh); Historical Society of Oak Park and River Forest (Diane Hansen Grah, Frank Lipo); Historical Society of the Nyacks (Winston C. Perry Jr.); Historical Society of Palm Beach County (Debi Murray); Illinois Division of Insurance (Sue Anders); Indiana University Medical School Library-Indianapolis; Indiana University Purdue University-Indianapolis, Library (Brenda Burk).

And thanks also to: Indianapolis-Marion County Public Library (Matt Hannigan); John D. and Catherine T. MacArthur Foundation (Richard Kaplan); MacArthur Agro-Ecology Research Center/Buck Island Ranch (Patrick Bohlen, Dan Childs, Gene Lollis); New City (NY) Library; New York University, Jack Brause Real Estate Library; North Palm Beach Public Library (Ann Burton), Village History Room (Joan V. Aubrey); Nyack College Bailey Library (Sunya Notley); Nyack (NY) Public Library, Local History Room (Betty Perry); Palm Beach County, Clerk & Comptroller, Record Service Center (Anthony Harr); Palm Beach County Library, North County Regional Branch; Palm Beach Gardens History Club (Amy Stepper); Real Estate Board of New York (Sean Lindstone); Saskatchewan Archives Board (Nadine Charabin, Christie Wood); Time, Inc. (Regina Feiler); University of Florida (Jim Liversidge); University of Nevada-Las Vegas (Tom Sommer, Su Kim Chung); University of Wisconsin-Madison (David Null).

The following individuals helped in a variety of ways: Elizabeth Brown, Ernest Theodore Brown II, William H. A. Carr, Phil Catasus, Jr., George Charbonneau, Claire Crawford, Katie Doubler, Robert Elmore, Ralph Girard, Bob Graham, Barbara Graymont, Marshall Gregory, Valiska Gregory, Carl Henn, Jr., Anne Hollister, Robert Hunter, John Irvine, Skip Lange, Phil Lewis, L. Robert Lowe, Jr., Billie MacArthur, Edward (Sandy) MacArthur, John R. (Rick) MacArthur, Joan Malick, Margaret Maxwell, Mary Maxwell, Madelyn K. Nasser, Roger E. Nixon, Gayle Pallesen, Leonard Pass, Edward Riguardi, Cory Ser-Vaas, Ardon Smith, Steve Steffel, John F. Taylor, Daly Walker, Margaret Winter, and William Lie Zeckendorf.

Though many who are part of the MacArthur mosaic have provided information, this book is an independent biography with no connection to or financial support from the MacArthur Foundation, the MacArthur family, or MacArthur business interests, past or present.

My special thanks to agent Ed Knappman, who believed in this book, and to the talented people at AMACOM Books who made it a paper-and-ink reality, especially Jim Bessent and Christina Parisi. I am particularly grateful to my terrific AMACOM editor, Adrienne Hickey, who provided wise counsel and an encouraging and steadying presence throughout the many months of research, rumination, and writing that a biography requires. And, of course, my thanks as always to the members of my family, who good-naturedly coped with a distracted writer and even came up with innovative ways to get dinner on the table.

"What counts in a penny is not its pedigree but its destiny."

—Advice from Professor Graham Taylor to critics who said
Chicago Theological Seminary should not accept money
from controversial John D. Rockefeller, Sr.

William Telfer MacArthur = Georgiana Welstead
1861 – 1949   1857 – 1915

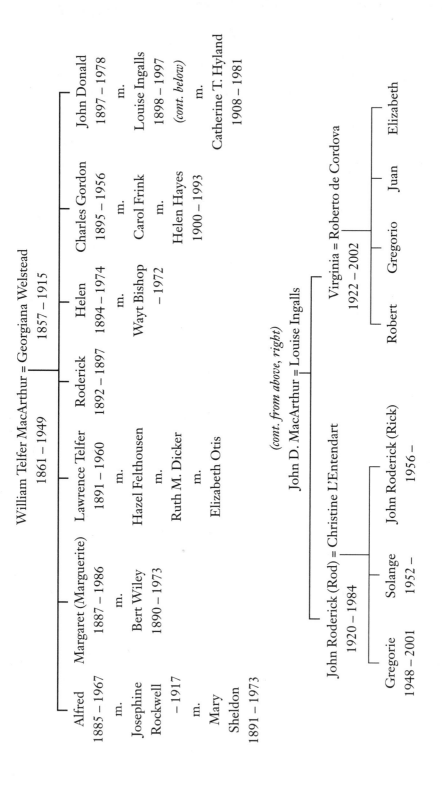

Alfred
1885 – 1967
m.

Josephine
Rockwell
– 1917
m.

Mary
Sheldon
1891 – 1973

Margaret (Marguerite)
1887 – 1986
m.

Bert Wiley
1890 – 1973

Lawrence Telfer
1891 – 1960
m.

Hazel Felthousen
m.

Ruth M. Dicker
m.

Elizabeth Otis

Roderick
1892 – 1897

Helen
1894 – 1974
m.

Wayt Bishop
– 1972

Charles Gordon
1895 – 1956
m.

Carol Frink
m.

Helen Hayes
1900 – 1993

John Donald
1897 – 1978
m.

Louise Ingalls
1898 – 1997
(cont. below)
m.

Catherine T. Hyland
1908 – 1981

(cont. from above, right)

John D. MacArthur = Louise Ingalls

Virginia = Roberto de Cordova
1922 – 2002

Robert   Gregorio   Juan   Elizabeth

John Roderick (Rod) = Christine L'Entendart
1920 – 1984

Gregorie   Solange   John Roderick (Rick)
1948 – 2001   1952 –   1956 –

PROLOGUE

I **STAND IN** a Florida parking lot in late afternoon, waiting for the phone to ring. If I move slightly to the left and look off toward the west, there it is, the iconic Florida scene: a tall palm tree silhouetted against an orange sherbet sky, bending slightly, gracefully toward the large ball of sun that squats, briefly, on the horizon. Click, goes the camera in my head. My cell phone remains quiet.

I am not surprised, actually, and anyway the party to which I have carefully *not* been invited is probably breaking up about now at the hotel bar three miles away. I had smiled, cajoled, turned on what I hoped was disarmingly innocent Midwestern charm, as I came right out and asked to be allowed to attend this annual ritual of "hoisting a glass or two" in memory of John D. MacArthur.

Though I knew that it was a long shot, this research trip had been arranged to coincide with the March 6 birthday of this complicated, controversial biographical subject whom I am trying to understand. John MacArthur has been dead since 1978, yet the residue of his Florida cronies (a thinner number every year) gather annually on his birthday to toast his memory.

Who else has people still gathering annually to remember them nearly thirty years after their death? A few dead presidents, perhaps, and religious figures, but hardly anyone else, even the most saintly among us. This is one more important fact about the man whose life refuses to unfold in straight, comprehensible fashion.

"But why won't they let me come and just observe quietly from a corner?" I asked one of the more approachable of these cronies. "They don't trust you," was the reply. And of course, I could not promise that I would buff out the less admirable episodes in their friend's life.

Nor could I promise others (often family members) who found the man distasteful that he would always be portrayed as evil incarnate rather than as a shrewd, colorful eccentric who, while always looking for the main chance, generally stayed just this side of the line—whatever the line. It's a description, incidentally, that could be applied, with modifications, to some of the others who piled up staggering fortunes in the nineteenth and twentieth centuries. MacArthur, at least, did not have the blood of the Homestead riots on his hands (Carnegie), or hire a public relations expert to pretty up his ruthless image into that of a benign philanthropist (Rockefeller). John MacArthur was what he was.

Many years ago, when Isabel Brookings turned over the papers of her husband, Robert Brookings (founder of the Brookings Institution), to his biographer, she asked only that he tell the truth. There is no better mandate for any biographer.

CHAPTER 1
RANSOMING THE RUBY

IT'S A THURSDAY afternoon in early September 1965, a sultry Florida afternoon. A man in the phone booth at a gas station plaza answers the ringing telephone. Trucks roar by on the nearby Sunshine State Parkway. The man reaches up above the door jam, feeling with his fingers. There it is, something smooth and hard—larger than a pebble—in a crevice atop the narrow ledge. It is right where the voice on the telephone said it would be.

He pulls it down and it winks at him—the wink of a clear, faintly pink star with six spindly arms, shimmering and shooting out light from the surface of a claret-colored stone the size of a large, luscious grape. He hands the gem to a stooped, gray-haired man standing outside the phone booth. The older man wraps the stone in a rag that he retrieves from their nearby car. That older man is John D. MacArthur, and he is paying $25,000 to ransom the DeLong Star Ruby, audaciously stolen ten months earlier from the American Museum of Natural History up in New York City.

Headlines in the *New York Times* identify him as "Florida Man . . . ," as if neither the *Times* nor its readers have heard of him. And many of them haven't, even though at this time he is probably one of the country's five wealthiest men. Quickly, newspaper readers learn much more—that MacArthur is the brother of the late playwright Charles MacArthur and, therefore, the brother-in-law of Helen Hayes, beloved leading lady of the American stage. That he has made his fortune in insurance (notably with a Chicago-based company called Bankers Life and Casualty) and real estate. That his reputation is spotty, to say the least, with past state and federal charges of fraud and "alleged wrongdoing"—but "no convictions," emphasizes one New York paper.

An hour or so after its pickup in the phone booth, the ruby lies on a table in Room 454 of a modest hotel in the modest town of Palm Beach Shores, on Singer Island, just north of the original Palm Beach. The Colonnades Hotel is a meandering collection of white buildings tacked together by arched colonnades. MacArthur, who owns the place, not only has an apartment here but frequently does business at his "office," one of the small, square Formica-topped tables in the hotel coffee shop. But this afternoon's transactions need a bit more privacy. In the hotel room a jeweler with a loupe announces that this is indeed the real thing. MacArthur, a bottle of bourbon in his pocket and the ruby in a bank sack, is hustled off to the First Marine Bank in neighboring Riviera Beach. He is obviously enjoying the whole thing. He shows the gem to reporters, flipping it into the air like a ten-cent lucky piece. (Somewhere in the Great Beyond, there's a gasp from Edith Haggin DeLong, the Manhattan dowager who gave the 100.32-carat ruby, mined in Burma, to the museum in 1937.)

In MacArthur's entourage as he arrives at the bank are his wife, Catherine, and the bank chairman and his wife. Though the banker is in dark suit and tie, MacArthur, peering down at the aggie-size ruby in his right hand, greets this historical moment in Florida mufti—an open-neck, short-sleeved sports shirt. It's not inappropriate. After all, there's a strong saltwater-and-sand whiff to this whole saga, this jewel-heist caper, as a novelist, say, Elmore Leonard or Carl Hiaasen might call it. But this is not fiction. And no novelist could invent a character more complex than John Donald MacArthur.

In 1965, at the time of the ruby ransom, he is one of only five living American billionaires: H. L. Hunt, Howard Hughes, John Paul Getty, MacArthur, and Daniel K. Ludwig. By the time of his death thirteen years later in 1978, MacArthur will be the largest private individual landowner in the state of Florida and probably the second-richest man in the United States, after shipping tycoon Ludwig.

The fortune he amasses will fund one of America's great philanthropic foundations, the John D. and Catherine T. MacArthur Foundation. In 1979, it will enter the ranks (and rankings) of American foundations at number four—behind the Ford, Robert Wood Johnson, and Andrew Mellon foundations, and ahead of the Rockefeller Foundation (number seven) and Carnegie (number thirteen).

The foundation's annual, high-profile, half-million-dollar MacArthur "genius awards" (more formally, the MacArthur Fellows Program) will recognize and support talent in amazingly diverse fields. Its funds will also support a worldwide variety of projects, from human rights education in Nigeria to research into how children learn in the digital age. Yet, at the beginning of the twenty-first century, though any man or woman on the street will be familiar with the names Carnegie, Rockefeller, Ford, Mellon, and Gates, the name and story of John D. MacArthur will remain essentially unknown.

John MacArthur was a brilliant, brash, nervy, shrewd businessman who would skate up to the edge of rules and regulations. He hated lawyers but was always suing someone. He neglected his own children, though friends' children found him fascinating. He could be rough and coarse, a bottom pincher, yet nearly three decades after his death, a loyal cadre of friends would still gather on his birthday each March to toast his memory.

MACARTHUR HAD BEEN pulled into the ruby drama in the first place by a pretty, brunette real estate broker who knew a writer researching a possible magazine series on famous jewelry thefts. The writer claimed he had stumbled across information that the ruby was being held as collateral for a Miami underworld loan. The loan had to be paid off before the ruby could be released, hence the need for Mac-

Arthur's money. Curiously, MacArthur, who could keep business executives squirming and biting their nails as they waited in his hotel coffee shop office or on the phone for a decision about whether he would lend them money for a shopping center or New York skyscraper, quickly agreed to jump into this cops 'n robbers drama.

The trio of thieves who committed the original burglary had been tagged by the newspapers as Florida "beach boys." Most colorful of the three was Jack "Murph the Surf" Murphy, former violin prodigy turned surf shop owner turned cat burglar. Daring and skillful in the execution of the theft of twenty-six rare gems from the museum, the thieves (who may or may not have been inspired by the movie *Topkapi*—depending upon whose later account you read) turned out to be incredibly inept during the days following the theft. Their wagging tongues and big spending landed them all in Sing Sing a scant six months after the burglary. After their arrest, nine of the twenty-six stolen stones, including the star sapphires Star of India and Midnight Star, were recovered from a Miami bus station locker, but the DeLong Ruby had already been swallowed up by the Florida underworld of fences, loan sharks, and con men.

"Here's Ruby" crowed the page-one headline in the New York *Daily News* the morning after its safe recovery. While the museum decided how to transfer the gem back to New York, down in Florida MacArthur let the citizens of South Florida get a look at the treasure. More than a thousand people filed by the stone displayed on a white satin pillow in the bank lobby, including one woman who was allowed to kiss it (for photographers) since it was her sixty-fifth birthday.

Saturday the ruby was finally ready to go home. Now on hand at the Florida bank was the American Museum of Natural History's assistant director (a robust Merchant Marine Academy graduate) who officially identified the ruby. "If it's the wrong one, I'll kick you in the pants," joked MacArthur. Hastily typed documents were signed authorizing the bank to transfer custody of the gem from MacArthur back to the museum.

By early afternoon the DeLong Ruby, accompanied by the museum official and a private detective, a black briefcase handcuffed to his wrist, were on a commercial flight headed back to New York. A crowd of reporters was on hand at JFK when the plane arrived, and another media mob awaited the pair on the front steps of the museum. While the noisy attention of whirring TV cameras and shouted questions focused on the detective with the briefcase, the museum official quietly walked around to a courtyard and entered the museum through a back door. The briefcase was a ruse. The ruby had traveled all the way from Florida over the museum official's heart, in a white plastic case under his shirt, kept in place by his bent arm.

The next day, Sunday, September 5, 1965, was one of those crisp fall days in New York that composers write songs about. An estimated 10,000 people streamed into the halls of the gray, Gothic museum across the street from Central Park on New York's Upper West Side to see the DeLong Star Ruby, safely home again. It lay on black velvet in a bulletproof glass case in the J. P. Morgan Memorial Hall of Gems, along with its two corundum cousins, the Star of India and Midnight Star sapphires.

MacArthur gave the ruby to the museum, said the newspapers. Period. Nothing expected in return, even though one observer in Florida had commented (probably facetiously) that maybe it should be renamed the MacArthur Ruby. It would not be, of course. John MacArthur had mentioned that he would probably claim a tax deduction for the $25,000. He was "very frugal," said a friend.

As it turned out, MacArthur later did accept the museum director's invitation to come up to Manhattan for a private thank-you luncheon, along with his famous sister-in-law, Helen Hayes, a museum patron. There was one problem. MacArthur, who was frequently getting sued, forgot that he had been avoiding the state of New York because a disgruntled former employee was suing him. As he, Catherine, and Hayes left their hotel to head for the museum, he was greeted by a process server. Helen Hayes ended up attending the museum luncheon in his behalf.

In Florida later that fall, MacArthur testified in federal court against the Miami underworld figure who had been arrested in possession of some of the ransom money—in marked bills. "The Government is very optimistic about their case. If they are successful we can feel we have made a contribution to society," MacArthur reported in a letter to the museum. The Bankers Life company magazine quoted a smiling MacArthur as saying it was purely a question of "public service."

Contribution to society? Public service? To MacArthur, money was to make, not to spend. Perhaps more to the point, therefore, was a story about a meeting MacArthur had with a group of Bankers Life ad executives sometime before the ransom negotiations were made public. A cocky bunch, they claimed the company's recent strength was the result of their advertising and requested a magnum budget increase. Well, said MacArthur, he would show them just how much good national publicity *he* could generate for just $25,000—and the eventual ransom publicity was indeed an advertising/PR bargain.

Even if impressing others had ever been part of MacArthur's game, who was still around to impress with this magnanimous gesture? MacArthur had long been out of touch with his daughter and had erratic relations with his son. (Decades later, one author writing about foundations would wryly point out that one reason the John D. and Catherine T. MacArthur Foundation was so well endowed was partially because MacArthur, "estranged from his two children for many years . . . transferred very little of his massive fortune to them in the form of lifetime gifts. . . .")

So who was there left of impress? Helen Hayes, of course. As a patron of the museum and other New York City cultural institutions, she would surely look with favor upon this selfless action by her sometimes embarrassing brother-in-law, who was not above taking advantage of her fame to market some of his Florida real estate. His wife Catherine? Not likely. Though the threatened divorce action of a few years earlier had been smoothed over, she knew him too well to be impressed—or surprised—by anything he did.

His mother had died when he was seventeen. His father, that harsh, strong-willed, charismatic evangelist—paradoxically kind (to his flock) and a bully (to his family)—was dead now also. As for his brothers and sisters—that amazing hatchling of talented, hard-driving individuals—two of his brothers also had died (Charlie at age sixty; Telfer at age sixty-eight, John MacArthur's age now). Elder brother Alfred, his nemesis, was in poor health. It was Alfred who had taught John the insurance business. But Alfred disapproved of his brother's shady business practices and scornfully told him he would never succeed on his own—ironically goading him into proving him wrong. By now, John had well surpassed the multimillion-dollar fortune made by his ailing older brother, who lived in a Chicago suburb and who had lost the ability to speak after a recent stroke.

As for his sisters, beautiful, cheerful Helen MacArthur Bishop, a onetime model now in her late sixties, was showing early effects of Parkinson's disease. Marguerite, the only one of the siblings to follow their father into a religious profession and who would outlive them all, was living quietly in a small town in Illinois.

They had made their way up from a painfully impoverished childhood, this brood of four boys and two girls. Yet if they had been raised in poverty, they were also raised in "a home where discipline, hard work, and dedication to a goal were valued," points out the historian and author Barbara Graymont, who has studied the MacArthur family. "Although he [John] had turned his back on his parents' religion, he obviously absorbed their tenacity."

And so, long before there was a ruby ransom, long before the (well-filled) silk purse of the John D. and Catherine T. MacArthur Foundation evolved from the sow's ear of John MacArthur's riches, long before there were MacArthur genius awards, there were William T. and Georgiana MacArthur of rural Saskatchewan, Canada, the pair who produced John D. and his fascinating collection of brothers and sisters.

CHAPTER 2

BREAKING THE SOD

THEY CAME FROM the East, answering the eternal siren call of gold. But the "gold" pulling the adventurous into Canada's vast prairies in the 1880s was wheat—green velvet carpets of timid shoots poking up from melting snow in early spring, ripening into shimmering fields of gold by late summer or fall. Wheat, settlers were discovering, thrived in the rich, loamy soil of the Saskatchewan Plain. Wheat varieties with names like Red Fife, Golden Drop, Odessa, and White Russian, some of which evoked sweeping grain fields in other rugged lands half-a-world away.

In 1884 young William MacArthur brought his bride, Georgiana, to their new farm tucked into the southeastern corner of Saskatchewan. This wild and open land, which the famed "Great Company"—the Hudson's Bay Company—had been forced to sell to the Canadian government a dozen or so years earlier, would not officially become a province until 1905. William, who lived in a tent on the land when he had first arrived two years earlier, had quickly built a small cabin, which was later joined by a stable and granary.

To claim a 160-acre homestead, settlers agreed to live on their land at least six months of the year and "break" (clear the land, turn the sod, and plant) at least ten acres a year. By the mid-1880s, the whistle of a train could be heard with some regularity drifting mournfully through the dark Canadian night. The Canadian Pacific Railroad was, after all, encouraging the settlement of the Canadian West. The grain milled from the wheat this fertile land produced would be loaded into railroad cars and shipped back to the hungry East.

The young couple settled reasonably well into the harsh, beautiful land. Neither was a stranger to the hard realities of farm life. Georgiana had grown up on the Ontario horse farm of her father, Alfred Welstead, a retired British Army officer. After the province of Manitoba had been opened to homesteaders, Welstead had started a new ranch there. William MacArthur, too, had grown up farming, first for his foster family back East and then as a farmhand for Alfred Welstead in Manitoba.

William Telfer MacArthur was born on June 18, 1861, in upstate New York, the son of Scottish immigrants. His parents moved to Canada, to the strong Scottish community of Galt, Ontario, where his mother died suddenly when William was seven. As the youngest of five children, William had been very close to his mother. (Decades later, at the end of his long life, William would be buried, as he had requested, in Ontario next to his mother.) When his father remarried, William, ten years old and apparently resentful, went to live with his mother's sister and her husband, William Telfer, for whom young William had been named.

The Telfers were farmers, and their household was sternly religious. William was expected to memorize ten Bible verses every week, and punishment was meted out for such misdemeanors as whistling on Sunday. Young William was seriously concerned about his salvation— even at age ten. "I found a little brass-bound Bible, with very fine print; its back was broken so it always opened at Job," he would write in his spiritual autobiography many years later. The book of Job was heavy going for a ten-year-old, particularly one who was a poor reader. His uncle's morning prayers were not much help. "The Scotch in those days were accustomed to use as many polysyllables as possible when addressing the Almighty," he wrote. One day when young William was pulling June grass from his uncle's potato field, he had a spiritual vision. The weeding was forgotten as he walked up and down the rows of potatoes saying, "I believe I am converted."

During his teen years, William MacArthur's interests vacillated between farming and the lay ministry. When he was about eighteen,

William left his aunt and uncle's farm and moved to Chicago, where he preached for a time for an evangelical and apocalyptic group called the Plymouth Brethren. A tall, handsome young man with wavy dark hair and piercing blue eyes, William was a good speaker and storyteller who liked a good laugh as well as the next fellow. Yet, despite his ease in public speaking and his growing abilities as a preacher, William was discouraged by what he saw as his own lack of spiritual growth. He decided to return to farming.

Among the friends he had made in Chicago was "another Christian young man," Charles Welstead, who would soon marry William's older sister Jane. Since Welstead's father, Alfred, was developing a farm in Manitoba and might need another farmhand, William made the trip with him to the family home in Ontario. It was a lively, cultured home, full of children. (Alfred Welstead's two marriages had produced a total of nineteen offspring.) William, adrift at an early age from his own family, seems to have fallen in love with the whole Welstead household, particularly the mother and one of the daughters.

Georgiana, born in 1857 and slightly older than William, was pretty, friendly, kind, intelligent, and well-read. She and her brothers and sisters were encouraged to use the family's large library, where they could read Dickens and other Victorian and classical authors. (Alfred referred to the farm's pigs as "Nicklebys," a funny reference to the greedy characters in the Dickens novel *Nicholas Nickleby*, who, like pigs at a feeding trough, elbowed aside anyone who might interfere with their gluttonous goals.) Alfred also insisted that his children read their Bibles every night.

Alfred hired the likable visitor, and the two boys headed west to the Manitoba farm. For William, however, bone-wearying farm work did not totally smother the urge to preach, and the small farming community welcomed the young newcomer who could lead frontier worship services.

In October 1883, William wrote Alfred Welstead from Manitoba asking for permission to marry Georgiana: "While in your house I was much taken with your family—though why my inclination was more toward Georgiana than any of the others I cannot explain." But the earnest swain added with a bit more grace, "I believe that Georgiana will be all that I could wish or expect to find in this world. The daughter of such a superior mother & father & member of what can (without any attempt at flattery) be called a model household. Beside these, there is what she is in herself. With God's approval and yours, I shall be satisfied." And he enclosed in the letter some spring wheat.

William, age twenty-two, and Georgiana, age twenty-six, were married in 1884 and headed for their new homestead in Saskatchewan, a scant twelve miles from the Manitoba border, not far from the Welstead farm and her brother Charles. A year later the babies began arriving. First came Alfred, born June 20, 1885, and named for Georgiana's father. In later years there seemed to be some uncertainty about whether Alfred was actually born in Saskatchewan, or whether Georgiana had gone back to her brother's ranch to have her first baby. Indian women had helped with the delivery.

When baby Alfred was about six weeks old, a party of Indians arrived at the farmhouse and came inside to examine the food supplies and load up on staples such as sugar and tea. Georgiana and the petrified neighbor women who were visiting made no objections. Then their leader picked up the baby and asked how old he was. (Later family legend suggested that the leader of the Indian party was none other than Sitting Bull, the Sioux chief who had led his followers to Canada after the battle of the Little Bighorn. However, this was highly unlikely since at about that time Sitting Bull, who had returned to the United States, was appearing in Buffalo Bill's Wild West Show.)

Whoever the Indian leader was, his attention to the baby thoroughly frightened Georgiana, who feared that little Alfred would be kidnapped. She explained that the baby was small because he had been born with the umbilical cord around his neck. The chief smiled and handed the baby back to his mother. The boy would see many winters and have many ponies, the chief said reassuringly.

But those winters were not to be in the Saskatchewan Valley. "Fortune . . . did not favor us," William MacArthur sadly would explain later about his four years of farming. The MacArthurs and their young son left the wilderness and moved back to civilization, this time Rochester, New York, where William was determined to try the ministry again. But after one year he still considered himself a failure. I will never preach again, he told Georgiana. He would go into business, he decided.

The couple's second child, a daughter, was born April 4, 1887. The new baby was named Margaret, after Georgiana's mother, though years later Margaret would fancy it up to "Marguerite." In the fall of 1888, three-year-old Alfred was hospitalized for six weeks with typhoid fever. The day before little Margaret's fourth birthday, a third child, Lawrence Telfer, was born. That was three children under six. Wrote Georgiana in her diary, ". . . he is a nice pretty black-eyed baby, but I am so tired I could almost say I want no more."

In the next six years four more babies arrived. Roderick was born in 1892 or 1893 and Helen, probably in 1894. Before Georgiana could catch her breath there were two more—Charles Gordon MacArthur, born November 5, 1895, and the seventh, John MacArthur, born a year and a half later.

CHAPTER 3

BABY JOHN

JOHN DONALD MACARTHUR was delivered by a midwife named Emma in West Pittson, Pennsylvania, on March 6, the first Saturday in March 1897. His mother was forty. He would be her last baby. It was just as well for she was already trying to cope, and often not too happily, with six other children under the age of twelve. In large families there is often an old baby and a new baby. When John arrived, little Charlie, at sixteen months became the old baby.

If the eldest had been a girl instead of Alfred, it might have been easier for Georgiana in some ways. The harried mother might have had more help with the younger children and the unending piles of clothes to be scrubbed and mended. On the other hand, with William—"Papa" now in her diary—gone frequently, Alfred at eleven had been chopping the wood for the household for several years, a not insignificant contribution to the family's well-being during cold Pennsylvania winters.

The MacArthur family had moved first to rural northeastern Pennsylvania, then to Scranton, and finally fifteen miles south to West Pittston. Pittston and West Pittston sat astride the juncture of two rivers whose euphonious Indian names—Susquehanna and Lackawanna—tumbled from the mouth like their waters tumbled down the valleys of the eastern Pennsylvania mountains. This was coal country, gritty and sometimes dangerous. Some years before the MacArthurs arrived, seventeen men had been killed in the explosion at Eagle Shaft, one of the historic coal mine disasters in this anthracite region. The *Wilkes-Barre Record Almanac* for 1897 matter-of-factly listed 111 names of men from the Pittston-Wilkes-Barre region who had been killed in the mines during the year. There was undoubtedly appreciation in the area for men of the cloth who could put sorrowing families in touch with the Almighty.

WILLIAM MACARTHUR, HAVING undergone yet another dramatic personal religious experience on the streets of Chicago when he was working as a traveling salesman, was now back in the pulpit again. "Pulpit" symbolically, that is. It was a term too grand for the front parlor of the house-church in Scranton where William first joined an evangelical group called the Christian and Missionary Alliance. This small Protestant fundamentalist movement would be his religious home from now on. His spiritual boat, at last, had docked.

William had come to Pennsylvania originally as an interim Baptist minister. "Lord, let me go," he had prayed. "I will preach to anyone, anywhere, for any price." One of his sisters, however, having attended a religious conference in Toronto, had sent William a subscription to *The Christian Alliance and Foreign Missionary Weekly.* The religious group had been founded by a onetime Presbyterian clergyman from Canada, Dr. Albert B. Simpson. Simpson had formed the new missionary-focused, evangelical movement after members of the staid Presbyterian church he was serving in lower Manhattan objected to the sometimes scruffy Italian immigrants he was bringing into the church. God was calling him "to a different work," decided Simpson, who began to minister directly to the throngs of immigrants pouring into New York in the late 1800s.

God, wrote Simpson, was "showing us a plan for a Christian church that is much more than an association of congenial friends [who] listen once a week to an intellectual discourse and musical entertainment . . . but rather a church that can be . . . the fountain of healing and cleansing . . . the sheltering home for the orphan and distressed. . . ." Hallelujah, said the restless William MacArthur in Pennsylvania, as he read reports in the weekly magazine of the activities, philosophies, and goals of the new group.

In 1896 at an Alliance convention, MacArthur at last had a private conversation with Simpson. The dynamic thirty-five-year-old preacher and the movement's founder talked until late at night. Simpson suggested that MacArthur move from Scranton, where he was the associate pastor of the Alliance's new Gospel Tabernacle, and set up a mission and church in nearby West Pittston. MacArthur was full of enthusiasm. According to the story Simpson later would tell, Mrs. Simpson, seeing the late hour, called for her husband to come up to bed. "Yes, dear," he replied, "I'll be up soon, but I've caught a rare bird this time."

It was a far rarer bird than Simpson could have known. William T. MacArthur was a paradox, almost in the biblical style of King David. This witty, spellbinding preacher, this imposing, magnetic leader from whose eyes blazed a determination to serve God, "counted success not in income but in terms of souls saved," historian Barbara Graymont would write years later. Yet William could leave his own family short of money and even food and ignore and belittle his work-worn wife. As adults the MacArthur children would still be trying to make sense of the contradictions in their father.

By far the darkest cloud to engulf the family occurred in 1897, just seven months after John was born. It was early October in the Pocono foothills surrounding West Pittston. An early, light dusting of snow lay on the ground. Three MacArthur children—Alfred, who was then twelve, and Marguerite, ten, pulling little Roderick (Roddy), five, on a sled— were roaming the countryside hunting chestnuts. The sweet, crunchy nuts were not only delicious snacks for the children, but any left could be cooked or ground into flour by their mother.

The children stopped at the neighboring Ferguson farm to see some young friends whose parents were also Christian Alliance members. For years there had been an old musket hanging on the wall of the Fergusons' parlor. Everyone, of course, (in those five most ominous words of any era) *thought it was not loaded.* But it was. The boys took the gun outside. Alfred playfully pointed it at Roddy and pulled the trigger. The old gun discharged, blowing off the side of the little boy's head. Another version of the story was that the gun was laid down and Roddy was looking down its barrel when it went off.

Marguerite ran outside and covered the dying boy with her dress, cradling him on the sled as they hurried back to town. A messenger rushed ahead to tell William and Georgiana the unimaginably horrible news. "The grief of the parents was pathetic indeed," said a newspaper account. Little Roderick MacArthur was buried in the town cemetery two days later.

And so baby John adapted to the rhythms of life, sleeping and eating, sleeping and eating. At eight months he was undoubtedly oblivious to the tragedy that had befallen his family, unless, in the wise ways of babies, he could sense a new tension in the arms of his weary mother. Unlike with Alfred, her firstborn, John's "creeping," his first teeth, his babbled first words went undocumented in his mother's diary. Unlike with Marguerite, his small hands and feet were not traced with a wiggly line on its pages. Unlike with Telfer, there was not a mention of the color of his eyes in the diary's increasingly infrequent entries.

But then the first child gets the lovingly documented baby book. The snips of baby curls and photos of the rest of a family's children often get shoved into a box (if they are saved at all). Just so, there is little trace of baby John (or Charlie) in the diary in which his mother had been writing since shortly before Alfred's birth.

The happy, excited young woman, whose first diary entry on May 20, 1885, began, "My dear Will, my husband, bought me this book and I am going to use it if all is well to tell about our baby that we expect God to send us soon," was writing entries with a sadder tone thirteen years later. Fatigue, rather than "dear Will," seemed to be her constant companion. After an evening religious meeting where the lesson was about the God of patience, she wonders "about Him being the God of rest." In another entry she writes, "Very tired and the children are so troublesome. Alfred is positively no good to take care of them."

Women in the small congregation came to call and brought food, and one offered to send over a woman to help with the household "and pay her." But there were other problems. "I do not know very much these days, everything is so strange," Georgiana writes in her final entry dated February 1, 1898. "My husband is positively nothing to me. He has not been home very much these last years and has paid so much attention to other people and I actually found myself jealous, yes, I did."

The entry continues: "There are lots of women he is so sympathetic to . . . and he seems so hard to me. . . . If I spoke of the children to him he said it was my duty to bring them up and that I had no government or management, that I was always complaining. Then the worst I got sick and he heard me crying and said I must die, the only way to make me was to give me a kick, and he gave me plenty." No one reading this years later can know if this troubling, obviously overwrought entry was meant figuratively or literally. The remaining pages in Georgiana's diary are blank. During her remaining twenty-five years, she never wrote in it again.

William MacArthur would go on to become a highly regarded, celebrity preacher within the Christian and Missionary Alliance, the man who inspired a young, wavering Billy Graham to regain his missionary zeal. Yet with all that, John MacArthur would say many years later, "I don't think he had as strong a character as my mother."

CHAPTER 4

LIFE WITH FATHER

THE SMALL BOY sat on a platform at the front of the religious gathering. On his neck was an ugly boil. Around him swirled a miasma of pain, hot lights, and emotional prayer. The Reverend William Mac-Arthur had become keenly interested in spiritual healing. Now seven-year-old Charlie's very visible skin eruption gave him a chance to dramatize the power of prayer over the painful ugliness of sin.

Georgiana's pleas were pushed aside. She wanted to be allowed to take the boy to a doctor, or at least give him the standard treatment of a hot poultice to bring the painful abscess quickly to a head and let it drain. For seven evenings Charlie sat on the platform, his little head bending in discomfort as the boil grew larger and the prayers grew more fervent. Finally the boil broke and the child was surrounded with much rejoicing and gratitude for this divine response. Charlie would have a puckered scar on his neck all his life as a souvenir of this episode.

Possibly there were other, less visible scars. John MacArthur, the little brother who saw his brother Charles in pain, would have been about five. Neither of these two younger MacArthur boys would ever show much interest in religion. In fact, of the six surviving MacArthur offspring, ironically, only a girl—Marguerite, the second eldest—would ever follow their father into religion as a professional calling. "I wonder if he [William MacArthur] ever understood his own role in this," a social scientist familiar with the family's story pondered many years later. "Today we know about the role of modeling in a child's learning about how to be an adult—how important it is for sons to have a male model to identify with, to relate to, one that is available and accepting." That, of course, was not how William would see it in future years. One time while preaching about Noah, he talked about how Noah kept his sons in line and "throwing pitch" to help build the ark. He added, as an aside, that if he had it to do over, he would have had his family members "throwing pitch more than they did."

BY NOW THE MacArthur family was living in Chicago, where they had moved in about 1901. William was serving as superintendent for the western district of the Christian and Missionary Alliance and also as pastor of the Gospel Tabernacle in the west-side neighborhood of Lawndale. The turn-of-the-century period of revivalist growth was producing what was called "muscular Christianity," male clergy members whose very identity was their rough-hewn vigor. Though their style brought men into worship services, their rugged authority was a particular magnet to congregations' female members.

William was a perfect fit for this new type of religious leader. His sermons and lectures, though properly biblical, were leavened with wit and innovation and were attracting more attention and attendance. But though his work as a pastor and as a preacher was increasingly successful, at home he could be a harsh father, a practitioner of the Old Testament philosophy that sparing the rod spoiled the child.

"When a writer is born into a family, the family is finished," the poet Czeslaw Milosz would write many years later. At the very least, cautions another adage, the family should be wary of the child who sits in the corner with paper and pencil and observes. (Not that the youngest MacArthur boys did much quiet sitting in the corner. Typical "preacher's kids," they were full of pranks and fun. William would often haul them to the front row of worship services so that he could keep an eye on them.)

Families should also be wary of the child who grows up and has literary friends who write down the stories the child remembers. In later years, Charlie would tell his pal and coauthor Ben Hecht hair-raising (and possibly dramatically embellished) tales about his father. "The Old Pollywog roared at us from morning to night," said Charles, according to Hecht. "He was constantly uncovering some new streak of wickedness in us. He would line us up at night, all hungry as wolves, beseech God in a firm voice to forgive us, uncover our backs, and whale the hell out of us. He kept a strap soaked in vinegar to make it a finer instrument of the Lord." Apparently, this punishment was meted out only to the boys.

Later in life, John didn't remember going hungry. The food was plain, he said, but there was always enough. But the scraping to get by, which exhausted his mother and made the family depend upon charity from members of whatever congregation their father was serving, those things John and his brothers and sisters remembered. William not only believed in the saintliness of ministerial poverty, but had written airily that "the Lord can be depended upon to finance any project that is pleasing to Him." Which, apparently, didn't always include dinner.

Over in Europe, Sigmund Freud was postulating a theory that later in life "the only happiness is the satisfaction of a childhood wish." The overarching childhood wish of the MacArthur children—of the three boys who became millionaires, at least—seemed to be to escape poverty. "I am not going to die poor," announced Alfred, as he stomped away from a missionary training institute in favor of a career in business.

Decades later, writer Stewart Alsop would scrutinize the lives of six extraordinarily wealthy Americans—among them, John MacArthur, along with Howard Ahmanson, Henry Crown, Edwin Land, John Mecom, and W. Clement Stone—and conclude that they all seemed to have some sort of "psychological burr under their saddles." In John's case, speculated Alsop, that burr was Alfred, "the rich and domineering older brother . . . whom John was determined to outpace." But it seems equally likely that poverty also provided some spikes on that burr. "In any case," wrote Alsop, "would-be Horatio Algers should be forewarned.

Without that burr—an obsession, magnificent or otherwise—they are not going to make it into the ranks of the new big rich."

ALFRED, HAVING SHAKEN off his father's career choice for him in the ministry, tried a couple of businesses before finally making the move, in about 1905, that would have profound repercussions not only for him but, as it turned out, for his youngest brother, John. He went to work for an insurance company.

Starting as a clerk at National Life Insurance Company in Chicago, Alfred rose steadily in the organization, impressing the company president, Albert M. Johnson, by spotting fraud at a flour mill to which the insurance company had lent money. Soon Johnson had another such job for Alfred. Several years earlier, Johnson had invested money in a gold mine in Death Valley supposedly "discovered" by a colorful character ultimately known as Death Valley Scotty—the "fastest con in the West." Alfred was sent out from Chicago to take a look at the mine.

After much random trekking around in the desert with Scotty, Alfred decided that there was no mine and that his employer, Johnson, had been hoodwinked. To put a stop to all this, Alfred confiscated Scotty's grubstake of horses, saddles, rifles, and binoculars. Scotty was furious and had Alfred thrown in jail. After about two days Alfred was released and made his report, but Johnson, it turned out, wanted to believe in the mine.

Through the years Johnson continued to support Scotty and eventually retired to a ranch in Death Valley, where he built an elaborate Spanish-style home with turrets and towers. Scotty was allowed to live in a primitive house on the property, though through the years, ever the con man, he frequently passed the elaborate main house off as his own. (In 1970 the National Park Service bought the property and "Scotty's

Castle" became a popular Death Valley tourist attraction.) The rest of Alfred's career in the insurance business, though very successful, was relatively prosaic compared to this colorful start.

By 1910 Alfred had married, and he and his wife, the former Josephine Rockwell, were living in the Chicago suburb of Oak Park. Eventually, the three other MacArthur boys, Telfer, Charles, and John, also would make Oak Park their home, at least for a time.

The early twentieth century was a heady time for the progressive village on the western edge of Chicago. Cultural, social, and religious groups were active and plentiful (though liquor was not—the village was "dry"). Education was highly valued, and Oak Park and River Forest High School was considered one of the best in the country. In Dr. Hemingway's large stucco house on North Kenilworth, young Ernest (the second oldest of the six Hemingway children) practiced the cello and later learned about writing short stories and newspaper articles in Miss Fanny Biggs's Oak Park high school classes.

The architect Frank Lloyd Wright had built a home in Oak Park and moved his studio there from Chicago in 1898. Though Wright himself had moved on by 1910, the homes and other buildings he designed for Oak Park clients left the village with many examples of his evolving Prairie School architectural concepts. In fact, Alfred and Josephine moved into the Wright home at the corner of Forest and Chicago avenues when it was first rented out in 1911. The studio had been converted into living quarters for Wright's estranged first wife, Catherine, and their children. Alfred and Wright would remain lifelong friends.

Telfer MacArthur, after finishing high school, also had stayed in the Chicago area. When the publisher of the small community publication *Oak Leaves* decided to reorganize his company, Alfred was named vice president and younger brother Telfer became business manager. The MacArthurs were becoming an important part of the Oak Park scene.

This left Helen, who was in high school, and Charlie and John, both in grammar school, living at home with their parents in Austin, a Chicago neighborhood to the east of Oak Park. Helen "was beautiful and loved by everybody," remembered a high school classmate later. Charlie and John, whom Georgiana had dressed alike when they were younger, were developing distinct personalities of their own. Charlie was a cutup, the prankster. John was a cutup too, but some considered him peculiar, different—a bit of "an oddball."

In 1911, with the older children off on their own (Marguerite had married a classmate from the Boone Bible Institute in Iowa), William and Georgiana decided to send their two youngest boys, Charlie and John, to a Christian Alliance boarding school in Nyack, New York. Wilson Memorial Academy had a two-year junior high school, the Preparatory Department (where John was enrolled), and four-year senior high school, the Academic Department (where Charles started).

Soon William was summoned east from Chicago to become associate pastor for the Christian and Missionary Alliance's flagship church, the Gospel Tabernacle in New York City. The senior MacArthurs moved to South Nyack (within commuting distance from Manhattan) and built a house on Shady Side Avenue not far from the school the boys were attending. Helen had stayed behind in Chicago with Alfred and his wife, so that she could finish high school.

Charlie and John lived a Tom Sawyer–like life in the small school settlement of buildings that spilled down the hills on the west side of the Hudson River, southwest of the Nyack village center. The MacArthurs' hillside frame house was modest, but the view across the river was spectacular. The boys helped with the carpentry for the new house and had started raising chickens in the yard until their mother put the breaks on the size of their flock by turning potential new stock into omelets. They were leaders of the neighborhood band of kids (to hear them tell it), and to hear everybody else tell it, they were generally full of mischief.

In the fall of 1913, William was appointed a field evangelist, which meant much travel and not much time at home. Georgiana had her hands full. "They needed their father!" a neighbor would later remember.

One time when William (apparently almost a stranger) did happen to be at home, he punished one of the boys, who promptly ran over to his mother crying, "That man hit me." Another time, Georgiana punished the boys by keeping them home from school and taking away their clothes as insurance. Instead, the two sneaked out to school—in their father's clothes.

Classes at the academy were demanding; the school's atmosphere was religious and student lives were carefully monitored. But Charlie and John, who roomed together while they were boarding students, still managed to pull plenty of high jinks. Once, John (known as Jack) was suspended for a week for crawling along a window ledge to get to the girls' side of the dormitory. Charlie, called "Chick," would sneak into nearby towns to sample such sinful diversions as movies and dancing.

Though Charlie was considered the student of the pair, John also did well at first, even if he was apparently less interested in academics. After missing two semesters of school because of illness, John still finished the 1912–1913 school year with a grade of 95 in algebra, an 87 in American history (always one of his stronger classes), an 85 in English, and an 84 in spelling—and a relatively decent B minus in deportment. On one occasion, John was called upon to recite in Bible class (not one of his best subjects). Having not prepared at all, John explained to the teacher that he didn't have a Bible. Why don't you tell your father you want one for Christmas, she suggested. If you think I should, I will, he replied after a pause, but I have never told my father a lie.

Charlie's literary and dramatic talents had already begun to surface. Occasionally he and John would pull down the shades in a dormitory room and surreptitiously put on a play for delighted fellow students. Charles, who served as vice president of the school's literary society, wrote so well that his father thought for a while that he had copied his pieces out of a magazine. John finished the equivalent of the eighth grade in 1913, the same year Charlie graduated from the Academic Department.

The year 1914 brought good family news from back in Illinois. Telfer married a young woman named Hazel Felthousen, and Alfred and Josephine had a baby, the first grandchild for the senior MacArthurs. The new little girl was named Georgiana, after her grandmother.

Marriages and babies notwithstanding, however, for seventeen-year-old John MacArthur, the big event during 1914 occurred along the Hudson River in the third week of July.

CHAPTER 5

THE COMPETITOR

NEVER HAS A river had a more poetically named source. Rising in Lake Tear of the Clouds—a small bog-like pool actually, high on the rain-soaked slopes of the Adirondack Mountains in upper New York State—a trickle of water becomes a brook, then a small river, and then the mist-shrouded Hudson River, flowing 300 miles to the south. Narrowing at West Point, it widens as it reaches Nyack like an anaconda digesting a recently swallowed goat.

Early Dutch settlers called this section of the river—three miles across at its widest point—Tappan Zee, sea of the Tappan (their name for a local Indian tribe). But the swimmer, head bobbing in the river that Monday in July 1914, was not thinking about the river's beauty or riparian history. Seventeen-year-old John MacArthur's focus was on the coveted W that had been offered for the past four years to the Wilson Academy student who successfully swam the Hudson. For the past four years the letter had gone unclaimed. John intended to change that.

Earning a school letter wasn't the only motivation. A week earlier a fourteen-year-old, swimming in late afternoon, had become the first girl (a girl!) to make the crossing at Nyack. Laughing at suggestions that she might be cold and tired, she waved at passing ferryboats and survived a heavy squall and four hours in choppy water.

For John, the weather was more cooperative. The air was calm. The Hudson's gray surface was gently dappled like a Seurat painting as John entered the river in late morning from the dock of the old four-story frame Tappan Zee Inn on Piermont Avenue at the foot of Mansfield. Two of the musicians from the hotel's orchestra followed along in a boat as a safety measure. Carried downstream by the tide, John reached Dobbs Ferry in two hours and "never faltered in his battle with the water," said the local paper the next day. "MacArthur," continued the newspaper article "is justly proud of his ability as a swimmer." The Wilson W was his.

John had finished his first year (1913–1914) at the Wilson Academy upper school or high school a month or two earlier. The first semester of upper school his grades had been good in three out of five subjects: American history, English, and algebra. But in zoology and Bible class, he barely scrapped along. He had dropped Latin, and in deportment he received a grade of D. In the second semester, again grades in history, English, and algebra were strong, but he had also dropped zoology and seemed essentially to have absented himself from Bible classes.

In September 1914, flush with the heady fame of the Nyack swim, he began his second year of upper school. But life at the MacArthur home was different. Charlie was gone much of the time, trying out haberdashery jobs in New York City. Alfred, Telfer, and Marguerite were all busy with their own families back in the Midwest. William was on the road, preaching and teaching. Most significantly, Georgiana had become ill, alarmingly so. Helen came to Nyack from Illinois to help look after her.

Partway through the fall semester, John dropped out of school, "either for lack of interest or because of his mother's rapidly deteriorating health," theorized family historian Barbara Graymont. Also, at seventeen, just ready for his second year in high school, John may have been embarrassed about dropping behind his age group. Though in later years there was talk from time to time about John going back to school, it was always too late in the year, or the semester had already started, or something. In essence, John MacArthur's formal schooling ended after his first year in high school.

Of the MacArthur offspring, only Marguerite had gone on to college or university (a Bible college), though Telfer had gone on to night school. However, none of the MacArthur children had stopped their formal education as early as John. Not that this was necessarily unusual for the times. Even if William had been able to afford a university education for his children—and Charlie probably showed the most academic promise—it was apparently beyond William to even think of encouraging any of the boys, particularly in higher learning that did not lead to the ministry, or more precisely, his own fundamentalist brand of ministry.

In the fall of 1914, Georgiana, gathering what little strength she had left, decided to plant tulip bulbs—a talisman of hope, perhaps—in the yard of the Nyack home on Shady Side. "The flowers will be up in the spring," she told Charles. "I'd like to see them." But it wasn't to be. The compassionate, civilizing center of the MacArthur family died February 15, 1915, of pneumonia, a month after surgery for intestinal cancer. She was not yet sixty. William returned from a preaching assignment in Springfield, Massachusetts, to visit her in the hospital in New York City shortly before she died. Not wanting him to know how serious her condition was (and possibly because she feared he would think her illness showed a lack of sufficiently strong faith), she had written letters for John and the other children to mail to him from Nyack. (John would later say that his father never upbraided him for his part in this well-meant deception.)

Georgiana's funeral, attended by "a large number of sorrowing friends," was at the Gospel Tabernacle in New York City. "She was a woman among ten thousand, strong in faith, loving in spirit, devoted to God and His service . . . ," said her obituary in a Christian Alliance publication. "She may well be counted the file leader of a host of Alliance women, who gladly sacrifice and pray and smile, in order that the gospel may be preached all round the world." She was buried with her parents and older sister in a family plot in St. Catharines, Ontario.

Shortly thereafter, William accepted a formal call from the Peace Chapel in Springfield, and he and the two remaining children, John and Helen, moved to the Massachusetts town. Helen was engaged to Wayt Bishop, a Nyack neighbor, and after waiting a respectable length of time after her mother's death, she and the young man were married. Now it was just John and his father. Since the semester had started, it was too late for John to go back to high school. Instead, he went to work for a company outside Springfield, learning to weld and making bayonets and sheaths, armaments needed for the war going on in Europe. On this side of the Atlantic, all of the MacArthur action had moved to Chicago—or so it must have seemed to John, now that Charlie had joined Alfred and Telfer out there.

"It's a fine thing to be a reporter. And young, and working in Chicago—1915," Charlie's friend Ben Hecht would write many years later. Maybe too fine a thing, worried William back in Massachusetts, when letters reached him with tales about Charlie's life in the rough-and-tumble, hard-drinking Chicago newspaper world. With Alfred and Telfer's support, John was able to convince his father that he too should head west, partly to be a steadying influence on Charlie. "Send him to me," said Alfred. Besides, William had decided that he was called to go back out into the field as an evangelist, and not having his youngest son at home would simplify things.

Telfer and his wife had been touring the East Coast and had come to visit William and John in Springfield. They would be taking the train back to Chicago. John, ever the competitor, decided to see if he could beat Telfer back to Chicago by car. A rich young friend of John's in Springfield had lent (or given him) a little Metz automobile (locally made in Massachusetts). Having been taught to drive a car by somebody's chauffeur in town, John, who was now in his late teens, jumped in the car and off he went—by himself. It was a long, tire-punishing drive through mud and over dirt roads, but the youngest of the MacArthurs finally made it. And possibly Telfer never even knew he was in a race.

In large families, generally the older kids help look after the young ones. So it was with the MacArthurs. Georgiana, with nineteen siblings and step-siblings, knew all about big families. It is not a stretch to think that she emphasized family helpfulness with her brood of six. Alfred had taken in Helen so that she could finish high school in Chicago. Alfred helped Telfer buy the community paper when its owner retired in 1916. Charlie moved in with Alfred and Josephine and baby Georgiana on Forest Boulevard in Oak Park when he first came west to work for Telfer at *Oak Leaves*.

Now it was John's turn. When he arrived in Chicago, Alfred took him in to live with his family in the Frank Lloyd Wright house. He also got him a job as office boy with National Life Insurance Company, where Alfred was now general agent for the Chicago area. (The Indian chief's long-ago prediction in Saskatchewan of "many ponies" for baby Alfred seemed to be coming true.)

John's new assignment consisted mainly of picking up and opening mail and, like many entry-level jobs, was boring, John decided. Soon he was selling a little insurance on the side—doing "fairly well," better than some of the older men, probably, he claimed later, because he worked more hours. Already John was chafing under Alfred's control. The twelve-year difference in their ages didn't give Alfred the right to tell him how to live, John decided. After a year or so, John changed brothers and jobs, moving in with Charlie.

In addition to writing for *Oak Leaves*, Charlie had worked as a reporter for the City News Bureau, the beginning rung on the ladder of Chicago journalism for many reporters. Charlie's big story, telegraphed around the world, was an account of the sinking of the *Eastland*, an overloaded cruise ship that rolled over in twenty feet of water in the Chicago River in downtown Chicago, killing nearly 850 people. Shortly thereafter, Charlie moved on to work for the *Chicago Herald-Examiner* and later the *Chicago Tribune*.

When John moved in, Charlie got him a job as a newspaper copyboy. Pretty soon John was a cub reporter, getting a $5 raise to $20 a week and working as a "legman," the reporter who calls in details about stories to the rewrite desk, where Charlie or another writer would turn the details into a bona fide story. But John himself realized he was not a newspaperman. His journalistic talent and interest in the newspaper business was minimal ("too much liquor and too little money" he would remember later).

Meanwhile, Charlie, always up for a little excitement, had joined the Illinois First Cavalry and was off "to the border" as part of General John Pershing's Punitive Expedition, giving chase to the Mexican revolutionary Pancho Villa. Villa had made a raid in 1916 on a small border town in New Mexico. A hero to many Mexican peasants, Villa was wreathed in legend by American newspaper coverage. The Punitive Expedition itself added to the cache of colorful stories—how one time Villa's soldiers, in civilian clothes, attended a movie along with Pershing's men; how Villa himself escaped the Punitive Expedition by hiding inside the body of a dead horse into which he had been sewn. These tales could rival even the growing body of Charlie MacArthur practical jokes.

Illinois Guardsmen, grumbling about the intense heat, the dust, and the lack of action, were not unhappy when, in 1917, President Woodrow Wilson ordered everybody home. Pancho Villa had not been captured, but the Illinois troops, like those returning to other states, got an enthusiastic welcome-home parade anyway. And it was while covering this parade that Ben Hecht, then a Chicago reporter, got his first look at Charlie MacArthur, with whom he would later collaborate in both work and play.

"Some hundred thousand citizens filled the sidewalks from Madison Street to Congress Street, waiting impatiently for a first sight of the sunburned militia and its victorious banners," Hecht would later write. The crowd was polite but confused when the first unit in the parade, far ahead of the bands and cavalry mounts, was an old car, zigzagging down the street. It was driven with one hand by a single soldier in uniform, waving an American flag and shouting unflattering things about the unit's colonel. It was, of course, Private Charlie MacArthur.

After his military arrest for this prank and confinement at Fort Sheridan on Chicago's north side, Charlie snagged a can of gold radiator paint and decorated his blue denim prison uniform with officers' insignia and epaulets, in preparation for a work detail policing a public area of scrap paper and trash. The colonel was not amused, though passersby were.

Younger brother John MacArthur had begun his own, one-of-a-kind wartime odyssey. The United States formally entered the war in

Europe on April 6, 1917, after a passionate, seventeen-hour debate in the House of Representatives that confirmed previous action by the Senate. The following month, John enlisted in the U.S. Navy as an apprentice seaman for a four-year tour of duty. He would last five months and three days.

On his enlistment records, John named Telfer as his next of kin and gave Telfer's Oak Park address as his home address. He (or the lieutenant at the recruiting office) also added two years to his age, listing his year of birth as 1895 instead of 1897. This made him twenty-two instead of twenty—for no good reason, since eighteen was the legal age of enlistment. The new seaman was of medium height and slim, five feet eight and one-half inches, 147 pounds.

But regimented service life was not for John. In early October 1917, a medical officer recommended that he be discharged, diagnosing his condition as "dementia praecox," the disorder that later would be called schizophrenia. "His conduct is bizarre," stated the medical officer's report. "He is impulsive and not reliable. He is indifferent to orders and he is emotionally unstable. Ambivalence and evasiveness are pronounced. He is erratic, seclusive, shut-in, and probably he is delusional. This condition existed prior to enlistment." Possibly. Or was this John, fed up with taking orders, *pretending* to be unsuited for military life, in some "bizarre" foreshadowing of the character Corporal Klinger in the television show *M*A*S*H* two wars later?

On October 24, 1917, Seaman MacArthur, being judged "not a menace to himself or to the community," was discharged into the custody of his brother Telfer. Telfer's daughter Jean would later remember that she was told that John, working as a milkman in Oak Park in about 1918, shortly before or after the end of the war, was "shell-shocked," a not-uncommon diagnosis in World War I, but generally for servicemen who had seen enemy action.

And John had, at least according to some of the elaborate and "bizarre" (to quote his Navy discharge) stories he would later tell magazine and newspaper interviewers about his military service. That, in his eagerness to see real action, he stowed aboard a troop train and was discovered and turned into a hero in a newspaper story written by a young female New York reporter whom he had dated. That he stowed aboard a troop ship, taking the identity of another serviceman, made it to England, flew a Sopwith Camel in combat, and was awarded the Croix de Guerre, which "were being handed out like popcorn."

The part of the story that can be documented is that after his abbreviated service with the U.S. Navy, John headed north to Canada and trained as a pilot with the Royal Flying Corps (RFC), which later became part of the Royal Air Force (RAF). According to John, a Canadian uncle, a brigadier general, helped him enlist. He, of course, did have Canadian family connections. His mother, Georgiana, often had gone back to Canada to visit her family during the summer, taking a child or two with her, so John was well acquainted with his Canadian relatives.

The RFC was desperate for pilots. John soloed after dizzyingly fast flight training. "If you had five hours [of instruction] and were unwilling to solo, you were immediately transferred to the infantry," he said later.

John returned to Chicago on leave, very much the dashing young aviator, wings proudly worn above his pocket and sporting a snappy mustache. You had to have a mustache to be an officer, explained John to Charlie. John was pleased with his new service branch. "You're like a knight of old. You go out by yourself and nobody can tell you what to do," said John, a telling comment from someone who had trouble taking orders, whether from a superior officer or an older brother. Another part of the story was that John became a flight instructor but crashed too many planes, the final crash occurring while he was training pilots in Texas. All that the sparse, official RFC/RAF records show is that by September 9, 1918, John Donald MacArthur, who flew the Curtiss JN-4, was "no longer physically fit for Air Service."

The war stories had calmed down a bit by the time John talked to a Miami reporter many decades later. "I was young and foolish and confused patriotism with adventure," he said, "and had a lot of fun."

CHAPTER 6

EVERY LITTLE BREEZE

LOUISE PEBBLES INGALLS had grown up in Oak Park, the daughter of a well-to-do family. After graduating from high school in 1916, she had gone off to the University of Wisconsin in the fall, enrolling in the school of letters and science. She was a quietly pretty girl, a brunette with large dark eyes who wore her hair in a stylish bob, bangs brushed low over her forehead. At Wisconsin she was a good but not spectacular student, on the staff of the yearbook, and a member of Pythia, a campus literary organization. She also went out for girls' baseball, though she didn't make the varsity.

She had known Marguerite MacArthur back in Oak Park, though she was several years younger—about the same age as Marguerite's youngest brother, John. Louise looked at John and perhaps saw Alfred and Telfer—stable, prosperous family men, leaders in the Oak Park community—but with an added frisson of excitement. With his dashing, wartime pilot persona—and the fact that her mother didn't approve of him—John must have seemed irresistible.

Louise was due to graduate from Wisconsin in the spring of 1920. Instead, she withdrew from school in the second semester and on March 17, 1920, ran off with John MacArthur to Valparaiso, Indiana, about an hour south of Chicago, where they were married. She was twenty-two; John had just turned twenty-three.

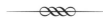

BY THIS TIME, John was again working for Alfred, selling insurance for National Life. He would go door-to-door in residential neighborhoods and hang out in factory parking lots during lunch hours, doing anything, going anywhere to sell policies.

Because of John's undeniable talent in the insurance business, the company president sent him to San Francisco to head National Life's California offices. John and Louise's first child, a boy, was born in San Francisco on December 21, 1920. He was named John Roderick, for his father John and for little Roderick MacArthur who had died so tragically in the shooting accident many years earlier. He would be known as "Rod."

By 1922, John was back working for the company in Chicago, and he and Louise had moved to Oak Park, where both had family living. John, Louise, little Rod, and baby Virginia (born in 1922) settled into a pleasant, spacious apartment with a sun porch looking out onto leafy Grove Avenue, lined, like many Oak Park streets, with majestic trees. All the MacArthur siblings were now married. Charles had married a fellow reporter and aspiring novelist, Carol Frink, in 1920.

Alfred's first wife had died in 1917 of goiter (an enlargement of the thyroid gland), leaving him with two young children, three-year-old Georgiana and a baby brother who was given the sturdy Scottish name of Robert Bruce. Alfred remarried in 1918. His new wife, Mary Shelton, a Chicago native educated at Bryn Mawr, was the sister of the well-known playwright Edward (Ned) Shelton. She, too, later became very ill from goiter, but medical treatment in New York saved her. (The Midwest, particularly states bordering the Great Lakes, was once part of "the goiter belt," the name given to those areas of the country where iodine, necessary for a healthy thyroid gland, had been depleted from the soil. Iodized table salt was not introduced until 1924.)

Personal tragedy continued to dog the life of the older MacArthur brothers. Alfred's young son Robert Bruce (Bobby) would drown. By this time, Alfred and family had moved from Oak Park to Chicago, where two more sons would be born, Edward (Sandy) in 1920 and

Alexander in 1922. Telfer's first wife also died (in 1922) when his daughter, Jean, was seven. There was a family pattern of not talking about these tragedies, at least to the children, realized Jean and her cousin Georgiana (Bobby's older sister), comparing notes in later conversations. "When my mother died, she just disappeared, that's all," said Jean many years later. In 1925, Telfer was remarried, to a widow with a young daughter.

The Reverend William MacArthur retired from active pulpit ministry in the mid-1920s, and to mark the occasion, his sons (there is no record of exactly which sons) sent him on a trip around the world. As he traveled across the Pacific in the spring of 1925, William did his best to establish a small religious beachhead on board ship, reading scripture to those who would listen, discussing evolution with the ship's surgeon and conducting occasional services at which the ship's orchestra played. "Alas and alack for the music!" wrote William in a series of descriptive, often witty, travel letters back home. Though hymnbooks were provided, the band's jazz musicians could not read music, wrote William, "but we struggled through."

In China, currently gripped by "a reign of terror," where many people "hated foreigners," William was struck on the chin by a rock while he and a Christian Alliance friend were riding a tram home from visiting the American consulate. Fortunately, his chin was protected by a beard. "The Scotch people in my boyhood always said that if anything was kept for seven years, a use would be found for it," wrote William in his travel letters. He had "cultivated" a beard for forty years, he pointed out. "The supreme blessing according to the Chinese traditions are first, sons; second, a beard; and third, wealth; but the greatest of these is a beard."

Before leaving America, William had been determined to travel as missionaries did, but a tortuous night in a third-class carriage on the train in India cured him of that resolve. Another goal had been to meet Gandhi, the "non-co-operation agitator," and a visit was arranged while William was in the ancient city of Ahmedabad. He found Gandhi squatting on his bed and not at all the charming, charismatic person he had expected. "If the mouth is an index of character, then his mouth is an unfortunate one. I could not determine whether it wore a smile or a sneer," he wrote. William and the Christian Alliance missionary accompanying him declined to address Gandhi with the customary title "Mahatma," because it "really means deity." This perceived discourtesy, William admitted, may have had something to do with Gandhi being "scarcely more than civil; certainly not cordial."

BACK HOME JOHN and Louise had moved into a house on Bonnie Brae, in River Forest, just over the Oak Park town line. John was demonstrating great success as a salesman. He worked relentlessly, sales call after sales call. He learned what worked and what didn't work when selling life insurance. He learned the euphemistic phrases for getting people to think about the unthinkable—that someday they would be dead. Gone. In a box in the ground. He was determined to make money to show them all—his increasingly successful older brothers, his uppity in-laws who thought he would never amount to anything.

Hard work might be admirable, but Louise wanted a more balanced, traditional life, with a husband who took the train home from the city at six o'clock every evening. Louise's family, suspecting that it wasn't always sales calls that kept John away at night, chose the dubious strategy of sending Louise's uncle to live with them, to try to help bring John into line. Uncle Harry decided to take Louise and the two children out to California for the summer to visit her grandparents. Autumn arrived, but John and Louise never moved back together again.

The marriage was over, in spirit and in fact, if not legally. John had spotted a cute, bright young secretary at the company who worked for his brother, Alfred. Her name was Catherine T. (for Terese) Hyland.

CHAPTER 7
CATHERINE T

SHE WAS SLIM, smart, attractive, and young—only in her teens when she first caught John's eye. The attraction, apparently, was mutual, enough so that this good Catholic girl was willing to hitch her wagon to a brash, fast-talking married man who would eventually get her to agree to a quickie, mail-order Mexican marriage after he claimed he had gotten a divorce. But then, even those with little else good to say about John MacArthur admitted that he was a terrific salesman.

Catherine Terese Hyland had begun working for Alfred in early 1927, when she eighteen and he was general agent for National Life. She was fresh from business school and it was her first job. The Hylands were a southside Chicago family. Just as Alfred Welstead had come from Britain and the MacArthurs from Scotland, the Hylands were another, more recent chapter in the story of North American immigration. Both Catherine's parents had been born in Ireland. Like many Irish immigrant girls, Catherine's mother had been "in service" to a Chicago family. James, her father, pulled himself up from day laborer to run, eventually, a successful real estate business and hold jobs under several Democratic administrations. One of his political jobs was superintendent of Navy Pier.

It was a big family—six girls, three boys. Several of the Hyland girls had college degrees and had worked for Alfred, both at the office and as vacation-trip tutors for his children. An older sister of Catherine's, who worked for Alfred at National Life, had become a high-producing Chicago insurance sales agent, unusual for a woman. Catherine, the sixth of the nine children, attended a parochial high school before going to business school. Growing up, she had been exposed to hard work, the real estate business, and the insurance business. It was perfect preparation for her future life, as it turned out.

A petite, pretty brunette with thin face and narrow, pointed nose, Catherine had more of a Gallic look than that of a rosy-cheeked Irish lassie. She "was an excellent business administrator," her youngest sister Patricia would observe many years later. (It was appropriate for someone with the middle name "Terese," since Saint Térèse of Lisieux was honored for, among other things, her organizational skills.) "He [John] was a risk taker. She, with her logical mind, was the brake on too risky ventures. Neither one could have made it alone."

John was now a part-time salesman for National Life, augmenting his salary over the next few years by driving a laundry truck route and operating a gas station in nearby Berwyn. Things were growing increasingly tense between the two brothers. It was more than just the developing liaison between the *married* John and Catherine (although Alfred, because of his established connection with the Hyland family, may well have felt a paternal responsibility for the well-being of the family daughters). For some time a basic disagreement had been festering between the two over the way the insurance business should be conducted. As far as Alfred was concerned, John would say anything to sell a policy. Too often policyholders would come to complain, saying, "Wait a minute. The man who sold me this policy said so and so."

The oldest and youngest sons of William and Georgiana seemed to have moral compasses set poles apart. Alfred was not one to shade what he saw as the truth. Not only had he insisted on telling his boss the truth about Death Valley Scotty—whether he wanted to hear it or not—but there was an earlier story in family lore. As a boy, Alfred, as the eldest trying to help feed the family, was working at a flour mill in the small Pennsylvania town where the MacArthurs were then living. While weighing the farmers' wagons he observed that some farmers had developed the trick of putting their wagons in certain places on the scale to register a heavier load. Alfred put marks on the weigh platform, hassling those farmers until they hit the new marks.

After a few days of this, the farmers complained. The mill owner pulled aside his young worker and told him to avoid confrontation and just put a finger under the weight bar on the loads of farmers who were cheating. The man with such a black/white code about phony gold mines and phony weights for farm wagons was not about to look the other way when he felt things were being misrepresented in his chosen field of insurance.

John, of course, remembered the parting a bit differently. During one of their arguments, John was getting a sermon from his older brother. "Alfred," said John finally, "I can work *with* you, but not *for* you." And it wasn't just Alfred. John's high-flying, lone-ranger style often bumped up against the entire company's restrictive (in John's eyes) procedures. One time, for instance, a big policy was declined, which meant a couple thousand dollars in lost commissions for John. Barging into a high-level meeting of the company's medical director and president, John tried to reassure them about the risk involved. After the medical director made a wisecrack, diplomacy went out the window (if it had ever been part of John's style in the first place).

"I've got news for you. You don't know how to run an insurance company," he said. "I'm going to build an insurance company, and if I fail, not only will everybody laugh at me, but nobody will hire me." With this parting shot—and challenge to himself—John realized he would now have to succeed. It was a sobering idea—"the honest belief that I could never get another job with an insurance company as long as I lived, unless I proved myself. A lot of times I was starting to throw in the sponge, but I was sure I had no place to go," the high-school dropout would remember later. "I could be a truck driver maybe, but that would be the end of my career."

Freedom from Alfred, but now what? When John left Alfred's employ, so did Catherine. By 1929, they both were working for State Life Insurance Company of Illinois, John as vice president in charge of sales.

Money is made by working in a field "where torrents of money are sloshing through and you can grab a handful as it goes by," an economist would observe many decades later. In the out-of-control boom days of early 1929, money was sloshing around in life insurance—maybe not torrents in the beginning, but enough to reward an almost desperate, dawn-to-midnight, hustling salesman like John MacArthur. But the title of vice president hadn't cooled off John, the smart aleck. Though two more years remained on his contract, the company's more staid and traditional directors were ready to see him go. "I'll make it easy for you," he told them. He knew that State Life was complaining about reinsuring a little company in downstate Illinois. MacArthur said he would go down and buy the little company if they would give him the money—and in exchange, he would release State Life from his contract. Buying a controlling interest in his own company was the only way to make any real money, he had decided.

LOVE—AND ITS complications—was in the air for MacArthurs elsewhere. Over on the East Coast, the late 1920s were turning out to be a pivotal for Charlie, too. In 1926, Charlie's first play had opened on Broadway. Though Charlie may have had much of the script done earlier, *Lulu Belle*, a melodrama about a black prostitute, became a collaboration with Edward Shelton, who was the brother of Alfred MacArthur's wife Mary. Ned Shelton was already an established American playwright, whose poor health now left him blind and bedridden. His contacts in the theater world were extensive. Charlie visited him frequently on Long Island, and Shelton became a friend and valuable mentor.

In the spring of 1928, Charlie and collaborator Ben Hecht were getting ready for the Broadway opening of their new comedy, *The Front Page*, based on the atmosphere, if not on the specifics, of their roistering days as Chicago newspaper reporters. When they were looking for a quiet place where they could work on rewrites of the play, Charlie had remembered his former hometown of Nyack, thirty minutes up the Hudson from Manhattan. They rented a ghostly old four-story building, formerly the Nyack Club, with some fifty bedrooms that was standing empty down by the river. Originally built as a boarding school for girls, it had later been a popular summer hotel, the Tappan Zee Inn—the place from which John MacArthur had made his swim across the Hudson fourteen years earlier.

The Front Page, with its wisecracking main characters "too scruffy to be heroes, too heroic to be villains," opened in New York on Tuesday, August 14, 1928, at the Times Square Theater. At another theater around the corner, the evening performance of the hit *Coquette* had been canceled so that its star, the popular young actress Helen Hayes, Charlie's fiancée, could attend the opening (the two plays had the same producer). *The Front Page* was an immediate hit. Three days later, on a Friday afternoon, Charlie and Helen were married.

The two had met several years earlier at a glittery New York soiree, awash in champagne and Jazz-Age celebrities. Helen, though a rising young actress, was relatively new to the world of theatrical café society. Somewhat ill at ease, she sat in a corner sipping ginger ale and watching Irving Berlin and George Gershwin vie for a spot on the piano bench and Algonquin Round Table wits like Alexander Woollcott and Robert Benchley try to top one another. Finally, she was approached by a tall, handsome man who, with what would become one the world's best-known pickup lines, asked if she would like some peanuts. Pouring some into her hand, he added, "I wish they were emeralds."

The incident, which had the brio of a scene Charlie would write, was apparently not apocryphal, and its frequent retelling would go on to haunt the pair. Decades later, bringing the dialogue full circle in Act III (like any conscientious playwright), Charlie returned home from India at the end of World War II with a small bag of emeralds. Dumping them in his wife's lap he said, of course, "I wish they were peanuts."

The afternoon wedding on August 17, 1928, was to be a small, quiet, almost secret affair in a lawyer's office on West Forty-second

Street, across from the New York Public Library. A judge would perform the civil ceremony. Though Charlie's divorce from Carol Frink had finally come through, it had not been a friendly resolution and there were concerns that she might try to roil the waters if the ceremony were too public.

At one point during their engagement period, Charlie had offered to see if his first marriage could be declared invalid so that Helen would not have to leave the Catholic Church to wed a divorced man. But that first marriage had been conducted by Charlie's father, William. Helen wouldn't hear of it. "Declaring Reverend MacArthur's ceremony invalid would have stripped the old man's waning life of all meaning," she would say later.

Now, however, as the time for the brief, civil ceremony approached, it was obvious that someone had tipped off the press, and the handful of friends (and Helen's ever-present mother) were joined by jostling reporters and photographers. After a wedding supper of lobster *diable*, the bride headed for the theater and her evening performance of *Coquette*.

Carol had fought the divorce for some seven years, despite years of separation. "I know of no other wife in the U.S. in that time who put up so fierce a battle to remain mated," Hecht would observe later. Actually, there was at least one. Louise Ingalls MacArthur would not officially be divorced from John until 1942, twelve years after they separated in 1930.

Months later, when the road company of *Coquette*, starring Helen Hayes, came to Chicago, Charlie took John backstage to meet his new sister-in-law. John was struck by her youth, though, in fact, she would have been at least twenty-seven. Having a famous actress in the family was nice, but John MacArthur was primarily focused on making his mark in the insurance business.

In early 1930, John took over controlling interest in that small, foundering company in downstate Illinois. The nine-year-old company had started out in Chicago in 1921 as Drexel Mutual Life, then changed its name to Monarch Life and moved to East St. Louis, Illinois. In June 1929, the company moved a bit north up the Mississippi River and inland to Jerseyville, Illinois, and again changed its name, this time to Marquette Life Insurance Company.

Catherine would later insist that she and John were actually equal partners in the venture, having agreed to pool their resources and earnings when they left Standard Life. Before new money was pumped into Marquette, the company had assets of $15.00, and the life insurance policies it issued were reinsured by other companies. A financial statement for December 31, 1929, showed a balance of $54.89. John contributed $2,145 to the company's surplus, appointed the president of the company as exclusive general agent, took over as vice president, and moved the company's principal office from Jerseyville to Room 1311 of one of downtown Chicago's renowned office buildings, the turn-of-the-century Marquette Building at 140 South Dearborn. The building's spectacular lobby was decorated with a mosaic frieze narrating highlights of Pere Marquette's 1674–1675 expedition into the North American wilderness, and sculptured bronze bas relief heads of Indian chiefs and French explorers over the elevator doors.

Marquette Life Insurance Company situated in the Marquette Building. Surely, it was not a coincidence. Choosing the name of a famous building to be the name of your newish insurance company was certainly a clever enough move to have been thought of by John. And if people thought it was your building, well, so be it.

But the country was plunging deeper into financial disarray, and by September 1931, struggling Marquette had moved into other quarters. Nearly a half-century later, in 1975, John MacArthur would buy the Marquette Building, the same year it was designated an official Chicago Landmark and a National Historic Landmark.

CHAPTER 8

STAYING AFLOAT

WHEN WALL STREET crashed in late October 1929, the insurance sector, like everything else, was nearly swamped by the resulting financial tsunami that gathered force during the early part of the next decade. John and Catherine worked frantically to keep Marquette Life afloat. The year 1930 "was the toughest," and 1931 was almost as bad, John would say many years later. "I was doing handsprings for hamburgers."

When the state insurance examiner came to check out the company for the September 1931 annual report, he found $10.28 in cash in the company's office, with an additional $893 in noninterest bank accounts. John, the only officer on salary, was theoretically paying himself $50 a week. An increase to $100 a week had been authorized, but "had not been paid to date," commented the examiner. The company did have a reinsurance contract with John's old employer, State Life Insurance Company of Illinois.

A few years earlier, Alfred, having left National Life in order to work on Herbert Hoover's successful presidential campaign (as did Telfer), had bought controlling interest in Central Life Insurance Company of Chicago, which later became Central Standard Life. Now Alfred, according to John, tried to get him to sell out before Marquette Life totally collapsed, so that the MacArthur name would not be associated with failure in the insurance world. John, of course, refused.

"I HAVE ALWAYS considered insurance to be one of the miracles of an advanced economic society," an industry historian would write many years later. Miracle, perhaps, but in its simplest form—that is, many pooling money to spread the risk of individual catastrophe—insurance was an ancient concept.

The Romans had burial insurance. The craft guilds of the Middle Ages offered artisans who worked gold into jewelry and wood into furniture not only burial insurance but also insurance against the particular disasters, such as theft and fire, to which their rough workshops were vulnerable.

Before the United States officially became a country, Benjamin Franklin had helped start a mutual fire insurance company in Philadelphia. A few years later, in 1759, Franklin also had a hand in the establishment of the first life insurance company in the colonies—begun by a church group, William MacArthur might have been interested to know. The name of the new organization was a mouthful: Corporation for Relief of Poor and Distressed Presbyterian Ministers and of Poor and Distressed Widows and Children of Presbyterian Ministers.

But more than Presbyterian ministers and their families needed protection from the exigencies of death—and life. Protection for business deals among the upper merchant classes (which lapsed when the deal was completed) and burial insurance for all classes eventually became available to more than just the membership of a specific organization.

In the early 1700s, the British astronomer and mathematician Edmund Halley had helped along the process of using science to determine insurance rates. After cataloging and counting the stars in the Southern Hemisphere (he found 341) and predicting the date of return of a great comet that would bear his name, he moved on to analyze the records of births and deaths in the European city of Breslau. The resulting mortality table showed the death rate over a year's time for various age groups. The mortality table, combined with development of probability theory in France, gave insurance companies something solid on which to base their rates.

The first company to use scientific data to figure rates was the Equitable Life Assurance Society of London, founded in 1762. Equitable Life in the United States was founded nearly a hundred years later, in 1859. Equitable Life was one of the big boys in the 1920s and 1930s, along with Mutual Life, Metropolitan Life, and New York Life. John MacArthur's Marquette Life was one of the little guys.

IN LATER YEARS, John would talk rather proudly about the chicanery of his early days in insurance. For instance, after opening the mail each day he would put it into piles. Checks would be taken from the pile of premium payments. The other pile, the one with claims, would be tossed into the wastebasket. Heck, if someone really had a claim, he figured he would hear from him again. (When this story was repeated to a claims department employee at Bankers Life and Casualty many years later, she visibly blanched. "I lived in terror that one of the claims on my desk would fall off into the trash basket," she said. "That would mean instant dismissal.")

A similar story John liked to tell concerned an insurance investigator who walked in the door one day with a list of thirty or so complaints about claims that had not been paid. They hadn't been denied, actually; they just had not yet been paid, since there was no money in the till. O.K., I will get these checks in the mail right away, John promised. Oh no, you don't, said the inspector. I'll wait right here while you write the checks and then mail the envelopes myself.

John walked over to Catherine's desk with the list and told her to write the first check and address the envelope—but he carefully moved his finger down to the next address on the list so that Catherine, but not the inspector, could see that the checks would not be going to the proper address. And so on, down the list. The time it took for claimants to return the incorrect checks and get replacements gave John enough breathing room to accumulate money from premiums to pay off. Only one person went ahead and cashed the wrongly made-out first check—and John sued him.

Leo Lahane was a friend of John's from the days when they both worked for Alfred, and for whom Leo still worked. Leo was a numbers guy. It was Leo whom John called after receiving some important news one Friday night in 1933. It seemed that Marquette Life was in the sights of the Illinois insurance examiner, who would be showing up the following week to see if the sickly company was still breathing. All weekend Leo worked on the books, preparing a financial statement. The verdict: Marquette had a miniscule surplus of $712.05. It was safe—for the moment.

CHAPTER 9

THE MOTHER LODE

ONE DAY IN 1935, a state insurance examiner dropped by John's Marquette Life office on Central Avenue on Chicago's northwest side. The message was not good. Insurance companies were still failing right and left. "The governor is going to put all you little guys out of business so you can't get a chance to swindle the people," said the examiner. And then he happened to mention a small three-year-old company, Bankers Life and Casualty, which had been referred to a liquidator just a few days earlier. Too bad, said the examiner. It was basically a sound operation, but it had been badly managed.

John bought the man a cup of coffee and learned more about this drowning company. For one thing, the man running it had been paying his own telephone and electricity bills with company funds, and there were other irregularities. By now, John was intrigued. When he contacted the chief examiner, he learned that the company's total liabilities exceeded its total admitted assets by $631.11. Just $2,500 would make it solvent.

What if I came up with the $2,500? John asked. Sure, said the examiner, who was glad to have one less company failure to handle. John again turned to Leo Lahane, who put up the $2,500 on July 1, 1935, and the receivership proceedings were dismissed the following day. Bankers Life and Casualty now belonged to John. This would become one of the standard John MacArthur ways of doing business: fire-sale purchases of distressed companies, followed by tireless efforts to turn them around. John moved Bankers into the Marquette office, took over as vice president, named Leo assistant to the president and C. T. Hyland (Catherine) assistant treasurer.

Though Bankers had two agents on the books, under new management it was again essentially a two-person operation: John and Catherine. John was selling. Catherine was running the office, doing the paperwork, keeping the books. But even as the company grew, she would always and forever be "Miss" (or sometimes "Mrs.") Hyland or "C. T. Hyland" on the letters and office memos she typed, even after a 1937 Mexican mail-order marriage made her legitimately a MacArthur (or so she assumed).

The previous owners of Bankers Life might have been financially feckless, but they did have at least one super idea, John discovered. At the time, $10 a month was generally the lowest premium the big insurance companies would accept. Companies needed it, their accountants told them, to pay salaries of officers and actuaries, and other expenses. "I had no overhead," John would say later. "I'd do business for what you had in your pocket—a dollar a month." Of course, after sizing up the farmer or carpenter or small businessman, John would mention that for just four dollars more ("that's only $5 a month") his quarry would have "a respectable thing here—not only can you get buried, but you can help your wife readjust."

For a while, John tried taking ninety-day notes if a prospect didn't have enough money. But that usually resulted in a bushel basket full of worthless notes. He went back to selling for what people had in their pocket. If a prospect looked like he had two dollars, he'd get a sales pitch for two dollars' worth of insurance. But the hard times weren't over yet. Truck drivers delivering coal to Bankers Life in the late 1930s were told not to leave a load until they had the cash in hand.

Not surprisingly, the rest of the insurance industry was appalled by this unorthodox newcomer. "I had a sort of a shyster operation in the eyes of the conservative people because I broke all rules," MacArthur would say later.

One of those rules he broke was selling policies by mail. Since John was essentially the only salesman, it had become clear that sales were limited by the number of sales calls he could cram into a day. He decided to turn his sales pitch into a letter, which was printed on simple newsprint (two dollars per thousand) and mailed to a thousand potential customers a week, along with a return envelope. The results were startlingly successful. Buoyed by this, MacArthur agreed to pay for a colorful, slick, professional mail piece that was again sent to prospects.

The fancy mailing piece sank like a stone. It was back to John's simple letter, and the money again began to roll in. To John's amazement, he suddenly had $70,000 in the bank. By 1941, Bankers Life had increased its life insurance in force to more than $20 million, a phenomenal increase from the $166,000 in force in 1935, when John had acquired the company. In the same period, admitted assets had risen from $5,802 in 1935 to $404,598 in 1941.

There was now enough money—and need—for John to expand the company's headquarters. In 1941 Bankers Life and Casualty bought a bank building at the corner of Lawrence and Kenneth avenues, about ten miles northwest of the Loop. It was located in Mayfair, a modest Chicago neighborhood of small businesses, small homes, and multiple residences that Chicagoans traditionally called four-flats or eight-flats, etc. The four-story building at 4444 West Lawrence Avenue was brick with terra-cotta trim and had tall, handsome brass doors and typical interior bank appurtenances of wood paneling and a large walk-in vault. Catherine's desk was up in front by the door so that she could keep tabs on everything.

During the next four decades, Bankers' Lawrence Avenue home would evolve into one of the most remarkable and unlikely headquarters of any major American company. Apartment buildings and neighborhood businesses—a florist shop, two grocery stores, a bowling alley—would be gobbled up, cemented to one another by the adhesive of John MacArthur's extreme frugality, and connected by a crazy, gopherden maze of ramps and winding halls.

The neighborhood funeral home across the street would become the personnel department (dead files were stored in the basement). Down the street, on the second floor above Little Joe's Tavern (still serving), would be the compliance and government-relations departments, where large, water-filled tarps hung from the leaking roof and nimble-footed employees dodged water buckets on rainy days. Wags called it "the rain forest."

John, constitutionally a tightwad, would take parsimony to new levels. Once he walked into a room where the office wall was being painted, an unneeded improvement, in his opinion. The painting was stopped, and the wall stayed half-painted for years. Even later, when he had money, he spent very little. Dollars saved would be the yeast, the seed corn, the grubstake for building the business.

This ongoing need for more and more office space was driven not only by Bankers' success (controversial though it was in some quarters), but by MacArthur's drive to snap up more insurance companies. In the early 1940s, in order to get equity in Bankers Life, MacArthur decided to change the structure of the company from an assessment or mutual insurance company (owned by policyholders) to a stock company (owned by stockholders). It was a financial Tinker-to-Evers-to-Chance operation involving Bankers Life and Casualty, plus an old company called Hotel Men's Mutual Benefit Association, and two other companies freshly minted for the maneuver.

In September 1942, a legal notice appeared in a Chicago-area community newspaper announcing the incorporation of an insurance company under the name Illinois Standard Life Insurance. Three months later, in December 1942, a certificate of merger was issued between Illinois Standard, "a stock legal reserve life company," and Hotel Men's Mutual Benefit, a "mutual assessment association." Illinois Standard (the stock company) was to be the surviving corporation.

There continued, in early 1943, a blizzard of reinsurance deals, resolutions, affidavits, amendments to articles of incorporation, mergers, and company name changes. When the dust (or snow) had settled,

Bankers, having conveyed all its assets, "including goodwill," to Illinois Standard, had changed its name to West Side Assessment Life Insurance Company, another new company, with John MacArthur as president. This left the Bankers Life and Casualty name and charter available, which was then assumed by Illinois Standard. West Side was dissolved seventeen days after its formation. Bankers Life and Casualty was now a stock company, and John MacArthur was, in essence, its sole stockholder.

No part of this maneuver was more useful than the merger with Hotel Men's Mutual Benefit Association. The key to the association's importance was the date of its founding: February 15, 1879. It was then that the first 102 names had been entered in neat, spidery handwriting into the Hotel Men's Benefit Association's large black ledger book. Hotel Men's members were assessed $1 a year for association expenses, plus $1 to $2 (depending upon age) for "mortuary purposes." Death benefits were $1,200.

A straight line in red ink was drawn through the name as members died. According to the Illinois Insurance Code, merged companies could claim the starting date of the oldest company. Like an ambitious New World matron who successfully makes a genealogical link to Old World aristocracy, Bankers Life (which was actually only ten years old in 1942) could now happily cloak itself in a reassuring patina of age. Bankers ads and letters began using the phrase "since 1879" and sometimes even the line "Chicago's First Insurance Company—Established 1879."

(More than a half-century later, Bankers would be much more transparent about its "founding" date. Explained a 2004 commemorative calendar celebrating the company's 125th anniversary: "The company known today as Bankers Life and Casualty was formed by the merger of three companies—Hotel Men's Mutual Benefit Association, Illinois Standard Life Insurance Company, and Bankers Life and Casualty Company. The oldest, Hotel Men's, was organized in 1879. Today, Bankers traces its history to that date.")

As he began to accumulate a bit of money, John decided to try using magazine ads to sell his bargain-basement policies. One magazine offered him a pretty good deal on $105,000 worth of advertising, but it was a no-cancellation contract. If the ads flopped, it would be all over for MacArthur. Again, he asked Leo Lahane for advice—and offered him a partnership. Lahane still turned down the partnership but advised John to take the advertising gamble. (Leo would finally join Bankers Life in 1949 as a well-paid executive, but not partner.) The ads were wildly successful. The first month's premiums alone paid off the $105,000.

Many years later, writer Stewart Alsop would use this story as an example of the difference in temperament "between the very special sort of man who becomes a great capitalist, and the much less unusual (but not necessarily less admirable or less happy) sort of man who becomes a respected and prosperous executive in a big organization."

According to Alsop, MacArthur remembered saying later to Lahane that he should have joined him as a partner at that time. No, said Lahane, "we wouldn't have made it as partners. I'd never have gone along with those ads." "But goddamit, you told me to go ahead," said John. "Yes," replied Lahane, "but that was your money. If it had been my money, I'd have said . . . don't take a chance. That's the difference between us."

Writer Alsop added his own shrewd observation: "Once you are rich, you can make a great deal of money with very little risk. But to become rich in the first place, it is necessary not only to have a good idea but also to go for broke to prove your idea will work."

IN THE 1940s Charlie MacArthur, nearing fifty, nevertheless went back to active service in WWII, this time as a major, then lieutenant colonel, and rather improbably as an assistant to the chief of Chemical Warfare Service. By now his drinking habit was legendary, and his pal Ben Hecht quoted a Hollywood wisecrack that Chemical Warfare's secret weapon was a plan to fly over Berlin holding Charlie by his heels and letting him breathe on the city. For Charlie "war was a place for wild frolic and a happy vacation from inner problems," wrote Hecht. "And it was the place where his old pal Death wore his most glamorous suit."

For the most part, however, it was the younger generation of Mac-Arthurs who answered the call to war this time. John's son Rod, who had been attending Rollins College in Winter Park, Florida, joined the American Field Service's ambulance service corps and served in France. Alfred's son Sandy, serving in the South Pacific in an IBM unit, was able to track down any serviceman in the area. He arranged a reunion with his cousin, Bill Bishop (son of Helen MacArthur Bishop), who was serving nearby on Okinawa.

A frogman as well as an actor-member of special services, Bill Bishop had been in a unit assigned the dangerous task of going into Okinawa ahead of invading U.S. troops to sweep the beachhead area clear of mines. When Sandy's unit moved on to Okinawa, he was able to see his cousin perform in shows put on for the troops. (Bill Bishop would go on to a postwar career as an actor in movies and television. Real-life mom Helen would even play his mother in an episode of probably his most successful comedy series *It's a Great Life*.)

The cousins—the three Bishop children (Bill, Bob, and Janet) and Alfred's three (Georgiana, Sandy, and Alex)—had known one another as they were growing up. Georgie would always remember that during one summer's visit, teenage Bill Bishop, the incipient actor, had been willing to read *Anthony Adverse* to her when she was recovering from a broken leg. But with often mercurial relationships between the four adult Mac-Arthur brothers ("they would be friends for years . . . and then nobody would be speaking to anybody," Telfer's daughter Jean would remember many years later), new kin would sometimes pop up out of nowhere.

One time, during a temporary thaw in relations between Alfred and John, Alfred called his children into the library of their home to make an important announcement: Their Uncle John was coming for dinner the following week. This was indeed a surprise, since they didn't even know they had an Uncle John. John showed up at Alfred's home in the tony Chicago suburb of Lake Forest—driving a dump truck. The dump truck developed a flat tire or some other problem, so John was driven home, having promised to send someone for the truck the next day. But the truck, looking very out of place, sat in front of Alfred's home for the next three weeks—just one of John's jokes on "stuffy" Alfred, the family decided.

Another time Sandy, who was driving through the East, had stopped in Nyack to spend the night with his aunt and uncle, Helen Hayes and Charlie MacArthur. To his surprise, a boy about his own age showed up later that day and they were introduced. It was an unknown first cousin Rod, John's son. On a bet with his father, Rod was seeing if he could take a road trip with no money—hitchhiking, living by his wits and off the "land" (i.e., friends and relatives). *Time* magazine, in its "People" section, had a different take on possibly the same escapade, claiming that it was "prankish, Cinemauthor" Charlie who had offered Rod and a college pal a trip to California if they got to New York on $2 and could wangle a night at a first-class hotel. The magazine ran a photo of the grinning boys enjoying an elegant room-service breakfast at the Hotel Astor.

In 1946, after returning from the war, Sandy had his own run-in with Uncle John. It seemed that a small, out-of-commission cement mixer sat in front of some property (a converted former convent) on St. Mary's Road outside of Chicago that Alfred had bought from John. Over and over Alfred told John to come and take the piece of equipment away. It was an eyesore, said Alfred, and needed to be removed since Alfred's daughter, Georgiana, now a widow, was going to be living there with her children. Nothing happened. Alfred threatened to send it to the junkyard. Nothing happened. Finally, Alfred told son Sandy that he and a young friend might as well fix it up and sell it. (In the years right after World War II, equipment like this was in short supply and therefore particularly valuable.) Alfred also suggested that Sandy and his friend get a new title to this piece of abandoned property, which the boys, to their regret, did not bother to do.

The boys spent hour after greasy, sweaty hour—weekends, evenings after work—overhauling the engine and making other repairs. Unbeknownst to them, however, either John or someone spying for him (they later speculated) was watching from the bushes as the work proceeded. Finally, the last coat of paint was applied and the mixer was ready for a weekend sale. The next day, while the boys were at work, a man showed up and told the caretaker that he had come for the mixer and hauled it away. "Well, you've learned a good lesson," Alfred said with a laugh. "Anybody who works with John MacArthur gets his fingers burned after awhile."

CHAPTER 10

DIVORCE . . . AND DEATH

LIKE THE DROP of water that finally makes the bowl overflow, something—possibly personal or financial or ethical—finally made Catherine say "enough." Early in 1948 she moved in with her sister, Patricia, who was now working for Alfred, and refused to see John. John asked Pat Hyland to intercede with her stubborn sister. "I can't do anything. She has a mind of her own," said Pat. It could have been that John's legendary roving eye had lingered too long in one spot. Comely young ladies who worked for Bankers Life were famously and forever warned about getting too close to the owner if they weren't willing to put up with gropes and pinches.

Or it could have had to do with John's attempt to retrieve ownership of Catherine's certificates for 133,000 shares of company stock. Or it could have had to do with mail fraud investigations connected with John's recent acquisition of Westminster Life. (John had been indicted, along with the previous owners, though he eventually would be cleared.) Or it could have had to do with other potential legal and tax problems hiding under rocks that Catherine, better than anyone, knew about.

The bombshell had been John's announcement, in March 1948, that their August 1937 Mexican mail-order marriage was probably not legal anyway, since his first wife, Louise, had never received any notice of a supposed May 1937 Mexican divorce. In that divorce action, John's Mexican attorney had stipulated that the marriage involved "no children nor property of any kind." Furthermore, Louise did not have legal representation (and possibly didn't even know about the proceedings down in the Mexican state of Morelos). John did legally divorce Louise in March 1942, in Calumet City, Illinois. This time Louise was represented by an attorney, and "children . . . both of age" were acknowledged in the proceedings. But this happened, of course, five years after the papers for his Mexican marriage to Catherine had been filed, describing *el senor John MacArthur* as *soltero*—single.

On April 23, 1949, a year after she had moved in with her sister Pat, Catherine was served with papers in a divorce action brought by John, charging desertion. This, apparently despite the ongoing question of whether John and Catherine had ever been legally married in the first place.

If John had thought that Catherine, this canny woman who had helped him on his upward climb, would go quietly into the good night, he was mistaken. A firestorm of complaints, answers to complaints, and new charges followed. As part of her legal team, Catherine had hired the firm of Stephen Mitchell, a local and national Democratic power (he would later serve as chairman of the Democratic National Committee from 1952–1955), and began lobbing some grenades of her own.

She countered the divorce action by saying that though she and the plaintiff had "lived and cohabited as husband and wife" since 1937, they apparently had never been married, as John himself had pointed out. Catherine and her lawyers then sued John, six Bankers Life officers, and Bankers Life and Casualty, the company, in a twenty-five-page complaint. The complaint asked, among other things, that Catherine be recognized as a full partner and the lawful owner of 500,000 shares of Bankers Life; that John transfer to Bankers certain funds currently run off the company books; that he repay the company for his Lake County farm and residence, cars, and private airplane; and that he generally straighten up and fly right. Perhaps the greatest twist-of-the-knife-in-the-heart to John was the stunning amount of detailed information the complaint revealed about his normally secretive business operations. Some family members, though no great fans of Catherine's, were delighted to see that in this instance, she had out-Johned John.

Take, for instance, the details revealed about a so-called App-Fee Account. This was an account funded by the one dollar that policyholders had to submit with every policy application. This App-Fee was, at John's direction, kept in accounts separate from regular Bankers' accounts, said the complaint. Funds so collected totaled more than $400,000 and had not been reported on Bankers' statements. More than $65,000 from this App-Fee account had been used "for the sole benefit, pleasure, or profit" of MacArthur, paying for his personal expenses and personal investments, continued the complaint. Moreover (and here the lights really began flashing red), some of these investments would not have met the rules set forth by the state of Illinois and Internal Revenue about what were appropriate investments for insurance companies.

The account was sometimes referred to as the "Employees' Welfare Account." From Catherine's complaint, it sounded as if the "employees" who primarily benefited from this account were John MacArthur and assorted cows and chickens. This was the account that had funded MacArthur's purchase, a year earlier in 1948, of a farm on Milwaukee Road in Lake County (in Chicago's upscale northern exurbs), plus livestock and poultry and a home across the road. The only benefit to the employees of Bankers had been a one-day company "outing" at the farm.

Back in the courtroom, the judge in the divorce action called John and Catherine into his chambers, saying this was a case of too much money and too many lawyers. He recommended that the pair go away together for a week and see if their differences couldn't be reconciled. On June 22, 1949, Catherine's charges against John and Bankers and the directors were dismissed. According to settlement agreements, John gave up claims on stock certificates held by Catherine and she gave up claims to full partnership in the company. Catherine's charges of mismanagement were also dismissed. "Lawyers indicated a settlement was made on the basis of a division of property," reported a newspaper article about the "surprise" settlement.

In September 1949, the divorce action of *John D. MacArthur v. Catherine Hyland MacArthur* also was dismissed. "He was really in love with her and she was in love with him, and even though it was a business relationship they were good friends," said her sister Pat, many years later. John on occasion would say that he owed much to that "wonderful" divorce court judge for making sure that he and Catherine stayed together.

DURING THE YEAR or two that John and Catherine were separated, John had begun spending many weekends in New York City. Often he would fly to New York in his own plane and stay at the St. Moritz hotel. "I don't know why—convenience, I guess," he would say later, as if he also was surprised to remember this period in his life when he embraced the expensive Manhattan high life. Though the hotel was elegant, the plane was not, at least in the traditional sense. A B-25, the twin-tail, twin-engine World War II workhorse had once been General Harold "Hap" Arnold's. With the armament removed and the bomb bays sealed, the plane was fast as scat. Conveniently, there was a one-time military airfield across the road from John's suburban Chicago farm.

An even more exotic piece of army surplus that was said to be in John's increasingly varied investment bag was Attu in the Aleutian Islands. Attu and Kiska (a neighboring island) had been the only U.S. territory to fall into Japanese hands during World War II. The postwar investment opportunity here was scrap metal from wartime battle that could be salvaged and resold.

Another unlikely investment, but one that jibed with John's frequent presence in New York, was the magazine *Theatre Arts*. In 1948, Charlie had taken over as editor of the thirty-two-year-old magazine, which had fallen on financial hard times, been combined with another magazine, *Stage*, and resurrected. Telfer's company in Illinois was handling the printing, and late in 1948, while in New York, John was dispatched to see why the publisher was not paying the printing bills. He and Charlie had dinner together, with John determined to convince Charlie that he should bail out and the publication, again in financial trouble, be allowed to take its final curtain. But Charlie's fabled persuasive charm carried the day. By the end of the evening, John had instead agreed to put money into the operation and take over as publisher.

Time did a story in its Press section entitled "Brother Act," pointing out that the masthead "now flew two MacArthurs instead of one" and calling the January 1949 issue of *Theatre Arts* a success. Continued the article, "'We didn't want anything with the MacArthur name on it to fail,' explained John loyally. 'My group—just some unpicturesque businessmen who want to make money—has put up $500,000 to make it go.'" The *Time* article was flanked by a two-column photo of Charlie and John.

One of Charlie's successful innovations for the magazine was to reprint a full play script in each issue, with Maxwell Anderson's *Joan of Lorraine* leading the way in the January 1949 issue. Rod MacArthur, who had stayed in France after World War II, had a three-page article in the next issue. It was an interview with Jean-Paul Sartre about the American adaptation of his play *Red Gloves*. John would write later that he "kept the magazine alive at considerable expense, until Charlie's death. My only profit was enjoying the companionship of Charlie and his friends."

With serious drinking taking up more and more of his time, Charlie was doing less writing for *Theatre Arts*, let alone adding to credits that had included cowriting the screenplays for such movies as *Gunga Din* and *Wuthering Heights* in the 1930s. He began work with Anita Loos and Ludwig Bemelmans on a possible play for Helen Hayes, but it was never finished. Over the next half-dozen years, his family and friends sadly saw him go downhill, in the company of what pal Alexander Woollcott had once called "that unhappiest of vaudeville teams—Haig and Haig." His health had deteriorated, and now his mind—the wit, the brilliance, the talent—was dissolving in a 100-proof fog of denial.

Ben Hecht claimed that Charlie drank both because he realized his antic youth was over ("growing old to him was like losing a leg") and to quiet the judgmental voices of his preacher father that still rang in his head. But then "every drunk has an excuse," John would say many years later. "Charlie's only excuse for getting drunk was Helen's success. He says, 'I go to a party' and they say 'Meet Mr. Hayes.' Perfect nonsense, but that was his excuse. . . . He wanted to drink." (Interestingly, in Nyack Helen Hayes always insisted on being known as Mrs. MacArthur.) John had lost patience with his brother's drinking, and this (in John's opinion) affected their closeness during Charlie's final years.

IN THE FALL of 1949, trees in the Hudson River valley burst into their usual spectacular oranges and reds, then shivered in the winds of approaching winter and dropped their leaves. Just so, glorious life and talent flared brightly in one of the younger MacArthurs, shivered in a sudden cold wind of illness, and then was gone.

Helen Hayes had been doing a tryout in Connecticut of the play *Good Housekeeping* with Mary, the MacArthurs' nineteen-year-old daughter. Mary, tired and suffering from what was presumed to be a cold, was sent home to Nyack and then, as her conditioned worsened, down to New York City, where she was placed in the hospital. As it happened, Charlie, whose ulcers had kicked up, was in the same hospital. The doctor's diagnosis was that word most dreaded by parents of the era: polio. (Jonas Salk's breakthrough polio vaccine would not be available for another six years.) By the time Helen reached the hospital, Mary was in an iron lung. She died shortly thereafter.

John had flown to New York and put his plane and crew at the disposal of Helen and Charlie. The most immediate problem, however, was that the medical authorities not only would not let Mary's parents see her body but insisted that the body be destroyed, a not uncommon practice because of fear of the contagion of the poliovirus. Helen was hysterical. John got in touch with some New York contacts and helped arrange instead for the coffin to be sealed and delivered to Nyack for a funeral the following morning. To have Mary properly buried in Nyack's cemetery was at least some little solace to her grieving parents. A year later, Charlie had carved upon her tombstone Ben Jonson's lines: *Here beneath this stone doth lie/As much beauty as could die.*

In November 1949, two months following Mary's death, another MacArthur died, but this death was not unexpected. The Reverend William T. MacArthur, who had been living in a retirement/nursing home in Warminster, Pennsylvania, died at the age of eighty-eight. Though John would later tell an interviewer that he was with his father the day he died, this was not the way personnel at Christ's Home remembered it. John had only visited once, they said, flying in and out in a day by private plane (though, with his brothers, he had contributed to his father's financial support at the home). Other family members— Alfred, Helen Bishop, Charlie, and Helen Hayes—visited more regularly. William's sons, in telephone conversations, decided to split the costs of William's burial. Only John did not contribute his share (according to the story told by Alfred's family). Charlie provided the information for the death certificate; Telfer and Alfred made the funeral and burial arrangements.

Nearly fifty years earlier, Georgiana, William's wife, had been buried in the Welstead family plot in St. Catharines, Ontario, near Niagara Falls. Though William, too, would be buried in Canada, the husband and wife would not be buried together. As he had often requested, William was buried next to *his* mother in Mount View cemetery in Galt, Ontario. Grandson Sandy MacArthur (Alfred's oldest son), who was working in Pittsburgh at the time, roared up to Galt in his open-top MG convertible, still a rarity in the late 1940s. There, he and other members of the American branch of the family gathered with their Canadian relatives (some of whom they had never met) for William's funeral.

In the latter part of his life, William MacArthur had developed a good relationship with several of his grandchildren, particularly Georgiana, the eldest grandchild. "As is so often true, absent fathers become good grandfathers," commented someone familiar with the family story. Most of William's children had softened in their attitude toward the father as they—and he—grew older. That is, all except John, whose "irreverence and bitterness" was still "evident" many years later when he was visited by representatives of Nyack College hoping to encourage a financial interest in the school with which his father had been associated.

CHARLES MACARTHUR DIED early in the morning on April 21, 1956. He had been hospitalized four days earlier for nephritis and anemia. The immediate cause of death, said doctors, was an internal hemorrhage. Friends knew, however, that his health had spiraled downward dramatically in the years following the death from polio of his beloved nineteen-year-old daughter, Mary. Helen Hayes was with her husband when he died. He was sixty years old.

Ben Hecht, his playwriting partner and pal from the roistering Chicago newspaper days, delivered the eulogy at the service in Manhattan two days later. "My friend Charlie, dying, leaves behind a thousand stories," he said. "He didn't write them all. He lived them all over the world. They were stories that added laughter and a sense of wonder to our Time. . . . His mind grinned at sham. He played tricks on everything pompous. And his heart stayed full of compassion for anyone in pain or misfortune."

"When he was young," said Hecht in closing, "Charlie used to sing a moody Scotch song. It echoes on his death—

"Bonnie Charlie's gone away

"Out across the deep blue sea—

"Many a heart will break in two—"

The final line, perhaps intentionally, was omitted.

Hecht would provide a eulogy with more Hollywood panache in his book, *Charlie: The Improbable Life and Times of Charles MacArthur*, written the following year. In it, he explained the origins of the phrase used frequently at movie story conferences: "Let's make the hero a MacArthur." An MGM producer who was a great fan of Charlie MacArthur's style and mannerisms had started it all. "I heard it in scores of conferences. It meant let's have a graceful and unpredictable hero, full of offbeat rejoinders," wrote Hecht. "Clark Gable, Spencer Tracy, Cary Grant, George Sanders, Robert Taylor, and a dozen others, including Jimmy Durante, 'played MacArthur.' The trademark of the character was that if somebody fired a gun he didn't look up, and if a woman was madly in love with him he amused her by sliding down a banister."

Charlie MacArthur was buried in the Oak Hill cemetery above the town of Nyack, where he and his adoring younger brother John had whooped and hollered and generally affronted (at least so they hoped) the community's stuffier residents. "I was guilty of hero worship and knew that Charlie could do no wrong," John would write a few years later.

IN THE EARLY 1950s, John MacArthur again had gotten involved in the New York theater world—he agreed to put up the money for Clare Boothe Luce's new play, *Child of the Morning*. Though he had put money in MacArthur/Hecht productions in the past, this time there was no family sentiment involved. Luce's play starred former movie moppet Margaret O'Brien, now fourteen and fresh from movie versions of *The Secret Garden* and *Little Women*, making her stage debut. Actor Eddie Dowling coproduced and directed—and stepped in to replace one of the original actors. The thriller-melodrama was about a saintly young girl (O'Brien) in an Irish-Catholic neighborhood in contemporary Brooklyn.

Tryouts were in Boston, where the play had a brief run at the Shubert Theatre. When it appeared the production was in trouble, John got in touch with a friend, the actor Burgess Meredith, who at first thought he could fix the production by taking over as director. When that didn't look practical, Meredith advised MacArthur to pay off the theater and shut down the production. Officially it was announced that the play had closed for rewriting, but it never made it to Broadway. The basic problem, said John later, was that the script, partly inspired by Clare Luce's conversion to Catholicism, broke the old show-biz adage that if you want to send a message, use Western Union. The play would get a brief "revival" in New York at Blackfriars Theatre in 1958, with one critic complaining about the young saint's "dreadfully jaunty American cheer." The jaunty American deep pockets of John MacArthur were probably not available this time.

John got involved once more with a Luce—this time the playwright's husband, Henry Luce, publisher of Time Inc.—in the run-up to the 1952 presidential election. He and Luce were among those (Texas oilman H. L. Hunt was another) parading into General Douglas MacArthur's spacious suite at the Waldorf Towers, trying to convince him to run for the Republican nomination for president. The general said no, according to John's retelling of the story to a reporter many years later, saying that he would rather go down in history "as a successful American soldier than as an unsuccessful politician."

John said that he sat with the general and others in a hotel room during the July Republican convention in Chicago, listening to radio reports from the convention floor, where General Dwight Eisenhower was winning over the more conservative Senator Robert Taft. John might have been listening in a hotel room, but he was not with General MacArthur. After delivering a surprisingly poor keynote speech, the general had decided to fly back to New York the same night, where he secluded himself in the Waldorf. ("The memories of convention survivors, muddled by exhaustion, are often unreliable," William Manchester would write many years later in his biography of Douglas MacArthur.)

Back in Chicago, throughout the evening the general's backers continued to talk of a Taft-MacArthur ticket, or even of Taft stepping aside after the first ballot in favor of MacArthur as a compromise candidate. That was never to be. Eisenhower won on the first ballot. "Think of what would have happened if MacArthur had been nominated," John mused later. "Taft was dead in a year and MacArthur would have been president. Things would be a lot different today." John MacArthur, it is probably unnecessary to point out, was also politically an ultraconservative.

Some of the MacArthurs still thought they had close, cousinly ties to Douglas MacArthur. This included Telfer, who had talked of the supposed family connection in his unsuccessful run for Congress in the late 1940s. As historian Barbara Graymont would later write, "Any possible blood relationship between the two families would be too ancient to be traced."

CHAPTER 11

HAT TRICK

JOHN'S SEEMINGLY insatiable taste for drama—the litigious kind—continued to be fed by Bankers' fights with federal and state tax authorities, state insurance departments, zoning boards, and anybody else who put up his dukes. In October 1951, the Illinois insurance commissioners convened a special hearing and invited representatives from the fourteen states in which Bankers Life was doing business. Obviously, John and Bankers Life executives were not the only ones who had carefully read the twenty-five pages of Catherine's earlier chancery suit.

At the hearing, four general topics were discussed: Bankers' record on payments; its unorthodox investment activities; an unreported employee welfare account; and the company's advertising policies, including its claim that its record of financial dependability stretched back seventy-two years. The latter claim, the only item to receive an official reprimand, was invalid, said the hearing's report, since two of the companies merged into Bankers had been insolvent at the time. "From this inquisition, MacArthur emerged virtually unscathed," *Fortune* would write a half-dozen years later.

But the Oscar for insurance drama surely would go to John MacArthur's three-year battle with the insurance department of the state of Georgia, which had begun even before the Illinois hearing. In July 1951, Georgia Insurance Commissioner Zack Cravey, no apple-cheeked innocent himself, announced that he had revoked Bankers Life's business license, since his office received fifteen or twenty complaints a week. (The company's White Cross health insurance plan had 260,000 Georgia policyholders.) Also, Cravey said, the company implied in its advertising that it was a nonprofit organization. The charges were "ridiculous," replied John MacArthur, as he filed suit in response. Cravey, like commissioners at the October 1951 Chicago hearing, also had concerns about the Bankers employees' welfare fund, it later appeared.

Six months later in January 1952, however, Georgia's Supreme Court issued a table-pounding opinion that government could not tell a company how to manage its business without the country being "plunged down the road to a socialistic state and the end of individual liberties." Bankers' Georgia license must be renewed. Shortly thereafter, Cravey pulled a different legislative act from his quiver and again took aim at Bankers. He claimed that this recent act did too give him specific powers and therefore reversed the decision of the state Supreme Court. Bankers could not sell any new White Cross policies, announced the Georgia insurance department, but policies now in force could continue.

In the meantime, Bankers Life officials had learned that Cravey was working with Florida and other state insurance agencies to curtail Bankers Life's operations. Sniffing a chance to prove conspiracy under the Sherman Antitrust Act, MacArthur dispatched Bankers Vice President C. F. Brusnighan to Atlanta late in the summer of 1951. A stenographer in the Georgia Insurance Department had agreed to supply copies of letters from the insurance commissioners in Tennessee, Ohio, Alabama, and Florida and a transcript of a June 1951 meeting in an Atlanta hotel. For these services she had been offered cash and a lifetime job with Bankers at a salary of "$325 a month." She had expected to meet MacArthur himself, but Brusnighan said he was in court in Ohio and couldn't make it.

In a scene worthy of a Charlie MacArthur movie script, Brusnighan (the Bankers vice president) met the woman in what newspaper stories would call "a dimly lit" Atlanta restaurant called Mammy's Shanty. She handed over an envelope and received a cigarette package containing five rolled-up $100 bills. The exchange signaled law enforcement officers and witnesses to materialize out of the dimness. Cravey, it turned out, had recruited her to play along with the bribe offer. Brusnighan slipped the envelope under the seat of his chair (restaurant chairs sometimes had special racks under them to hold men's hats) and indignantly informed the detectives that the money was to pay travel expenses for the stenographer who was coming to work for Bankers. Another colleague of Brusnighan's showed up wearing a big Stetson and, during the ensuing confusion, retrieved the envelope, hid it in his hat, and left the restaurant.

The envelope contained documents that, said MacArthur, proved collusion between Georgia's Cravey, Florida Insurance Commissioner J. Edwin Larson, and other insurance companies controlled by a Texan who, according to MacArthur, wanted to move in on Bankers' operations. In April 1952, MacArthur filed a $30 million suit, this time in a Miami court, charging three individuals and four insurance companies with conspiracy to force Bankers Life out of business in Florida and Georgia and asking for $30 million in damages.

There remained a slight problem, however. With the stenographer testifying for the prosecution, both Brusnighan and the Bankers agent in Atlanta were convicted in Georgia Superior Court in 1953 of causing the illegal removal of state records through bribery. Though this was a felony, the jury recommended punishment for a misdemeanor and the two men were fined $1,000 each and sentenced to a year in prison. A week later the sentences were cut, the motion for a new trial dismissed—and the Bankers executives, good thrifty MacArthur men all, asked the court to return the $500 that had been the evidence of the bribe. A year later, Bankers dropped its damage suit against Cravey.

Sometimes Bankers' image in the press was more positive. In 1953, Eleanor Roosevelt's popular newspaper column, "My Day," carried a lengthy item about a new quasi-governmental film, *America's Untapped Assets*, which had been previewed for United Nations representatives and others interested in "problems of rehabilitation." It featured Bankers Life and Casualty and the 650 "old people and handicapped people" the company had trained and employed. The film offered praise, noting that "the addressing machine is operated by a one-armed Korean veteran, and an eighty-year-old grandmother counts out millions of dollars in premium receipts."

Bankers Life had begun hiring the handicapped back in 1944, when World War II affected the supply of able-bodied men and women. With John, of course, there was often more to any action than what appeared on the surface. Cynics pointed out that employers often received government salary reimbursement for hiring the handicapped, including, much later in the 1970s, funds from the Comprehensive Employment Training Act (CETA). Even so, Bankers probably employed the largest number of nonindustrial handicapped workers in Chicago. Other employees learned not to trip over seeing-eye dogs and how to sign so they could communicate with fellow workers who were deaf.

There were some employees with limited mental abilities who, nevertheless, were well able to push grocery carts up and down ramps, delivering batches of claims and mail from one department to another. And sometimes Bankers' quirky headquarters itself facilitated this employment policy. In sections of the main building, basement ceilings were unusually low, only four and a half to five feet tall. Bankers was still able to make this usable space, however, by hiring dwarfs as custodians. It was an amazing sight, said employees, to see them marching through the building at night, gunnysacks of trash slung over their shoulders.

There was also no forced retirement at Bankers because of age. By 1954 more than a third of Bankers employees were over age 60 or physically handicapped, and *Look* magazine and the General Federation of Grandmothers' Clubs honored the company for these policies. (John MacArthur, Eleanor Roosevelt, and the grandmothers of America—indeed a fearsome combination.) MacArthur would always insist that these employment practices were just good business, not soppy do-goodism. "If they didn't do their job, they'd be fired," he said.

THE WHITE CROSS name had been chosen in the 1940s for Bankers' health and accident insurance plans. Not surprisingly, the Blue Cross and Blue Shield organization, whose Minnesota predecessor had first begun using a solid blue Greek cross in 1934, thought the similarity was much too close. Insurance commissioners in some states (for instance, Iowa in 1950) railed against use of the White Cross name. Later, Bankers was charged with trademark infringement (though when Bankers agreed, in 1958, not to register White Cross as a trademark, Blue Cross would drop the fight).

Typically, John MacArthur had only scorn for people who weren't smart enough to tell a White Cross from a Blue Cross. And though the White Cross name might be controversial in some quarters, it was proving to be an extremely popular symbol with Bankers agents and employees and was soon on its way to becoming the company logo.

Ads for health insurance in mass publications such as *Reader's Digest* ("What can you do about today's $75-a-day hospital costs?") featured a white cross in a circle, with the name Bankers Life and Casualty around the top and the year 1879, along the bottom. (Thank you, Hotel Men's.) Platoons of "White Cross men," as Bankers salesmen were sometimes called, would respond to the reply-card inquiries that the ads produced. Health insurance ads of the period were of serious concern to various government agencies, and Washington kept a wary eye on what companies, not just Bankers, were promising the public.

During the coming decades at Bankers, small white crosses would adorn the cuff links, tie bars, signet rings, notepads, paperweights, and cigarette lighters ("for a matchless salesman") given as incentive and promotion prizes. As John MacArthur well knew from his own years of knocking on doors, insurance salesmen, the load-bearing pillars of the industry, needed all the positive reinforcement they could get.

"For the insurance salesman, there are no easy victories; every day is a test of individual skill and perseverance," an article in a sales incentive magazine would say many years later. "Unlike salesmen in almost every other field, he never knows the excitement of a new model year, a new product, or a flashy advertising campaign that starts consumers clamoring to buy." Insurance agents, continued the article, "eke out their victories one at a time, sitting face-to-face in a prospect's living room, sipping coffee and alternating small talk with the grim realities of actuarial tables."

Bankers' management knew that besides grit, perseverance, and a certain glibness, another ingredient was key to a salesman's success—his wife. Wives of salesmen were entertained, along with their husbands, at banquets and parties recognizing those who met sales goals. At such a spring 1952 banquet in Baltimore (and probably repeated at similar events across the country), a vice president from the home office (the apparently indefatigable Brusnighan) gave a talk entitled "Salute to Wives." His text: A wife plays a major part in determining the success of her husband—and wives of "our men" could expect full paychecks only if their husbands put in full-time effort. His subtext: Don't grumble if your husband is out making sales calls every night, leaving you to oversee the kids' homework and scout meetings. You and the children benefit, too. Company publications would print photographs of smiling wives clutching envelopes containing "cash awards" if their husbands, for instance, had written more than $30,000 Life in one month.

In the spring of 1972, what would turn out to be a particularly effective company morale-building organization held its first annual meeting at a banquet at Chicago's posh Edgewater Beach Hotel. "Bankervetts" was the name chosen for this "seniority service club" for employees at the home office. Ten years with Bankers was required for membership. *Bankers Life*, a company publication, announced that henceforth "Bankervetts would be identified with an asterisk (*) in future issues."

In speeches, in company publications, there was always great emphasis on the Bankers "family." Most employees considered salaries good for the times. Teenagers who had a relative working for the company could get jobs after school for better pay than the local hamburger joint or drugstore offered, and later they could work nights while going to college. Young mothers could work the night shift in Adjusted Claims or Billing after their husbands on the day shift got home to watch the baby.

There were employee bands, singing groups, bowling leagues, and softball games at La Baugh Woods, a park just a ten-minute walk from the Lawrence Avenue home office. There were golf outings, picnics for all departments, and fancy holiday buffets that gave wives of salesmen and the girls in Corporate and Finance a chance to get gussied up in bouffant-skirted party dresses.

About once a year there were summer parties at John's aforementioned farm. With John as the host, these were, not surprisingly, frugal affairs but fun, remembered employees. At Christmas, "Mr. Mac" would stand at the back of a semi in the parking lot, helping hand out frozen turkeys to employees, many of whom then had to wrestle the big turkey box home at rush hour on the El or the bus.

Unquestionably, Bankers was paternalistic, but employees didn't seem to mind, though women were not allowed to smoke at their desks and for a while a series of bells signaled workers to be at their desks (7:58 A.M.) ready to start work (8:00 A.M.), just like high school. (Employee complaints finally got the bells removed.) And the company nurse, who gave shots and checked sore throats, occasionally would show up at the home of an employee who had called in sick, just checking. . .

Employees proudly put White Cross logos on their car windows, and there were white crosses on the side panels of the new fleet of small supply trucks acquired in 1952. But by far the most visible Bankers white cross was the one erected atop the headquarters building on Lawrence Avenue. Like a neighborhood sentinel, it sat atop a slim tower on the roof of the corner building. Running vertically down the side of the tower were the letters B A N K E R S, gleaming white at night from the light of the large, lighted, rotating cross above.

Not that the neighbors were overjoyed with their sentinel at first. Some of the company's Ward 39 neighbors, as well as city zoning authorities, had resisted when the company asked for a zoning exception so that new top stories could be added to the existing buildings. As usual, John got his way. A circuit court judge ruled that the zoning ordinance could not be used to stifle the growth of a company, "which is not in itself a nuisance."

Growth was the operative word. In 1943, Bankers Life was operating solely in Illinois, but by 1946 it had added four more states: Florida, Michigan, Missouri, and West Virginia, and by 1951 it was operating in fourteen states. In 1953, Bankers Life for the first time topped $100 million in premium income. To handle the claims and run the Addressograph machines to support this growth in this clerical-intensive, pre-computer era, the prewar home office staff of about fifty had grown to more than 2,000 by the mid-1950s. Increasingly, most of the North Mayfair neighborhood worked for Bankers. And if you didn't work there, you probably had a relative who did.

And so Bankers' neighbors got used to the light from the cross, this moon that never set. Summer and winter, the big white cross would revolve above Lawrence and Kenneth avenues until the day of a particularly fierce storm in 1974. High winds for which Chicago is famous swirled across Mayfair rooftops, lifting shingles, rattling windows, and knocking down the cross, which crashed through the roof. No one was injured, but the big cross was never replaced.

A phone call to Bankers shortly thereafter revealed that the insurance symbol had done more than just inspire salesmen. "Why did you turn the light out?" asked the official from O'Hare Airport. It seemed that pilots and the control tower had been using the large sign as a navigational aid.

CHAPTER 12

DOWN AMONG THE SHELTERING PALMS

THOUGH FLORIDA'S east coast escaped any major hurricanes in the mid-1950s, a different kind of turbulent force made landfall. John D. MacArthur foreclosed on several thousand acres of land, and Palm Beach County would never again be the same.

MacArthur, identified in a May 1955 newspaper article as a "Chicago financier," announced plans for a $20 million real estate development starting north of the modest town of Lake Park and extending south toward Palm Beach, along both sides of Lake Worth. There would be hotels, motels, and a yacht and golf club along the ocean, plus 6,600 home sites (half of them on the water). Lakes and rivers would be dredged. A sewer system and water plant would be built.

North of Lake Park the lots would have at least a seventy-five-foot frontage for homes that would cost a minimum of $10,000. Announced MacArthur's representative, "In this manner we believe that we can assure purchasers of high type people and eliminate the possibility of the property ever falling into bad repair."

The loan on which John had foreclosed had been made to Carl Byoir, the hotshot New York public relations man turned real estate developer, and his partners in the Palm Beach Development Company. And if MacArthur and Byoir were not a colorful enough lineage for this property, there was an earlier connection to Sir Harry Oakes. Born in America, Oakes had made a gold-mining fortune in Canada and moved to the Bahamas in the late 1930s. His bloody and sensational murder in Nassau in 1943—for which his son-in-law was tried and acquitted—

had riveted café society as well as ordinary newspaper readers, glad for a diversion from the latest World War II news.

Oakes had extensive real estate holdings in the Bahamas and across on the U.S. mainland dating back to the late 1920s and early 1930s. The "rises and falls" of the land in a certain section of the northern Palm Beach County "wilderness" appealed to him, and he had built a private golf course. In the 1950s, Sir Harry's widow decided to sell off some of these Florida holdings. It was this land that Carl Byoir and partners bought, financed by MacArthur, after he was given an aerial tour by helicopter of the extensive holdings.

The part of the Florida coast that MacArthur had looked down upon was still sparsely settled compared with what would come in the next decades. The few coastal towns—Jupiter, Lake Park (formerly Kelsey City), and fishing villages like Riviera Beach, with its Prohibition-era legacy of Conch fishermen whose money "catch" was whiskey not grouper—were separated by long open stretches of U.S. Route 1, sand dunes topped with sea oats, and palm trees. Those coconut palm trees—some said they were the result of a nineteenth-century shipwreck of a Spanish ship with a cargo of coconuts—had given the new county its name in 1909, when it was split off from northern Dade County.

With a population of some 115,000 in 1950, Palm Beach County, the largest U.S. county in total area east of the Mississippi, would nearly double in size to 228,000 residents by 1960. Two men and a war would help make this happen: John MacArthur, who had, in essence, stumbled into the area in 1955 when he foreclosed on Byoir; and Arthur Vining Davis, one-time chairman of Alcoa, who in 1956 would move his new real estate operations from Dade County up to Palm Beach County, particularly the Boca Raton area.

During World War II, servicemen stationed at airbases in Florida got a taste of year-round sun. At the war's end they were ready to bring their families down to paradise—and buy houses. "Half the people in the country would come to Florida if they could make a living here," MacArthur would say later.

This, of course, was not the county or the state's first land boom. Henry Flagler had extended his railroad down to the new resort of Palm Beach in the 1880s. But these guys were different from those who arrived, thrived, then sank in the 1920s, wrote local newspaperman Bill McGoun many years later. These new Florida developers "had become fabulously wealthy in other fields—wealthier by far than any of the 1920s giants. . . . When they bought land it was frequently by the tens of thousand of acres. When they developed, they developed not just cities but entire areas."

Not surprisingly, considering the personalities involved, relations between John MacArthur and Carl Byoir were not without complications. In addition to the Palm Beach County deal, MacArthur had provided Byoir and his partners, Ralph Stolkin and Julius Gaines, with mortgage loans for a housing development down in Carol City, north of Miami. John had signed a letter of agreement to take over development of Carol City, in effect another foreclosure.

According to MacArthur, he had cut off the cash flow to the Carol City builder (Gaines) because he didn't like how the money was being used. Gaines sued, claiming MacArthur actually just wanted to get his hands on Byoir's Carol City stock. Then Byoir circulated an affidavit quoting MacArthur as saying that he couldn't be intimidated by threats of a suit, since there were currently "3,000 lawsuits against Bankers, and this will just be one more." That does it, said MacArthur, and he filed suit against Byoir for $5 million to make him "stop libeling me."

(Some years later, MacArthur dropped his suit against Byoir's estate—Byoir had died of cancer in 1957—in exchange for the legal consideration of one dollar. In a classy, or maybe disdainful, gesture, Byoir's widow made her payment with a small one-dollar gold piece, which Catherine decided was half a pair of nice earrings. MacArthur had to ante up after all—for the earrings.)

MacArthur, had, of course, made occasional trips to Florida since the 1930s when Louise and the two children moved there from California. At first they lived in the Miami area before moving to Winter Park near Orlando, where son Rod attended Rollins College. "John did not believe in giving anyone a lot of money, but he made sure their needs were met," said a Winter Park neighbor and high school friend of Rod and Virginia's many years later. "I remember him driving down in 1939, in a 1938 Dodge which belonged to his insurance company. He gave it to them since they needed a car at the time." In 1942, Louise and daughter Virginia had moved to Mexico City after Rod went off to serve in World War II.

ONE OF MACARTHUR'S early forays into Florida land development left him walking away uncharacteristically empty-handed. MacArthur had approached Ernest "Cap" Graham, a politician and beef and dairy farmer, who owned about 6,000 acres north of Miami. One morning in the early 1950s, the two met in the bright, cheerful breakfast nook adjoining the kitchen of the Graham family's coral-rock farmhouse. Also at the table was young Bob Graham, grabbing a quick breakfast before catching the school bus to Hialeah Junior High. The young boy was used to these breakfast meetings. It was where his dad often discussed business and political matters. (These were good political seminars for the boy, who would grow up to be a state legislator, governor of Florida, U.S. senator, and briefly, a candidate for the U.S. presidency.)

John MacArthur had come to call because he wanted to buy and develop Graham's land. But first Cap Graham, making small talk, asked MacArthur to tell him about his start in the insurance business. MacArthur told him that story about the early days when he would open and sort the incoming mail into two piles and throw out the claims pile, figuring he would hear from those people again if their claims were legitimate.

After MacArthur left, "my dad, who was a fairly quiet, unemotional person, was as mad as hell," Bob Graham remembered later. "The man started out telling me he was a crook," sputtered Cap Graham to his son, "and then proceeded to try to get me into what would be the biggest financial transaction of my life. What kind of a fool does he think I am?" Needless to say, several decades later, when the Graham dairy farm was developed into the town of Miami Lakes by the Graham family, John MacArthur was not involved. During the next few years, property purchases by MacArthur, his front men, or his companies began showing up regularly in Palm Beach County's handwritten deed-record books. The MacArthur nose was sniffing out real estate deals elsewhere in the state as well. For instance, a trust of which MacArthur was the principal owner bought a large tract of ranch land (more than 32,000 acres) east of Sarasota from the Ringling estate for $25 an acre. However, northern Palm Beach County was the site of most of the MacArthur action—new houses in Lake Park and a whole new village, North Palm Beach, a bit further up U.S. 1.

Even John himself, now in his early sixties, just like many other Midwesterners of a certain age, succumbed to the siren call of Florida. He and Catherine began spending more and more time there, though Illinois would always remain his legal residence. In 1958, with housing construction underway in Lake Park, John and Catherine took a look at a model home and decided to move in. The modest bungalow in which the MacArthurs lived would have struck the wealthy of an earlier era—the Rockefellers and the Fords—as appropriate for "an under-gardner or a second chauffeur," visitor Stewart Alsop would write a decade later. "There is nothing in the house that might not have been bought from a mail-order catalog by any retired couple in modestly comfortable circumstances."

Not everyone was happy with John MacArthur's plans for Lake Park. MacArthur wanted to build water and sewage plants. The town fathers objected. MacArthur countered with a full-page newspaper ad calling them "unprogressive." When the mayor and other officials still wouldn't cooperate, he served eviction notices on the town's public buildings—which he owned. "I wouldn't have gone through with it," he insisted some years later, but the threat did the trick. Building of the water and sewage plants proceeded.

The people of Florida were, by now, getting the picture that this "Chicago financier" in scruffy clothes had more than ordinary financial resources. And in the fall of 1957, John MacArthur's financial cover was blown nationally. *Fortune* magazine published an article listing "America's Biggest Fortunes." The names attached to these fortunes were grouped in five categories, ranging from $700 million to $1 billion at the high end (of which there was one, J. Paul Getty) down to $75 million to $100 million (of which there were thirty-one, including "John D. MacArthur, Chicago, Bankers Life and Casualty Co.").

Even Chicago was surprised. "MacArthur Held Richest in Chicago" said a Tuesday morning *Chicago Tribune* article about the "furor" over his status as the city's richest man. Chicago's only other representative on the list was Mrs. Chauncey McCormick (Marion Deering), in the $100-million-to-$200-million category. But her listing carried the slightly pejorative notation (at least to American if not European sensibilities) that hers was inherited wealth, as were the fortunes of 55 percent of the people on the list. Though the article specifically listed by name only those with fortunes of at least $75 million, *Fortune* said it actually considered $50 million (in principal, not income) the bottom rung on the ladder of America's Very Rich, an "arbitrary" definition, the article admitted.

Nine photos ran with the article. The others were black-and-white photos, "but mine was in color," MacArthur would tell a reporter with some pride many years later. (Actually, four of the photos were in color.) MacArthur, looking rather natty in a light brown suit and modest tie, with plenty of white cuff showing, was "still keen to make more money," said the photo caption, and "has neither time for play nor appetite for living it up." This was typical, said the article. "It is hard to find an out-and-out hedonist, dedicated solely to self-enjoyment, among the . . . millionaires. The weight of $50 million seems to have a sobering effect on its possessors; it is really too big for frivolity, too kinetic for idleness, too conspicuous for privacy. Consequently, U.S. wealth is used, somewhat to the disappointment of the average American, for precious few eccentricities."

That last comment possibly indicated that magazine had not yet got the full flavor of MacArthur—his meandering, jerry-built insurance company headquarters, his extreme frugality, his frequently fractious and litigious way of doing business. That changed a year later. As MacArthur would later tell the story, in 1958, a *Fortune* reporter knocked on his door. The magazine, he said, had received so many letters questioning MacArthur's rank as Chicago's second richest ("what about Wrigley and Armour . . .") that the reporter needed to prove the claim.

With MacArthur's cooperation the reporter got his story, and in July 1958 the magazine "ran a special article on me only and not the other nine," said MacArthur years later, with some satisfaction. Possibly by then he had forgotten that the title of this new piece was "The Incorrigible John MacArthur," who, said the article, made his first fortune "in mail-order insurance, which dignified insurance men consider the demimonde of the industry." The article summarized his family history and whirlwind acquisition of other insurance companies. It outlined in colorful detail the lawsuits and investigations about Bankers' bookkeeping and investments, including the unorthodox purchase of 200,000 pounds of Parmesan cheese—which produced a profit of $22,500. "I'll admit more than you can prove," a confident MacArthur had once told state insurance examiners, said the article.

As to whether he belonged on the earlier *Fortune* list of $50-million men, the article calculated that, at the beginning of 1958, his insurance assets alone totaled $161 million. And that didn't include the new real estate action in Florida.

CHAPTER 13

BANYAN TREES AND HIBISCUS HEDGES

ONE—OR ACTUALLY three—reasons John was able to spend more time in Florida from the late 1950s on was the very capable triumvirate he had put together to run Bankers Life and his other affairs up in Chicago. There was good old reliable Leo Lahane, now a Bankers vice president, who had finally agreed to officially join the company in 1949, after having helped John through so many early insurance crises.

In 1952, Paul Doolen, a lawyer practicing in Lake County, had also joined Bankers as vice chairman of the board. He had represented MacArthur during a legal skirmish several years earlier. "I never thought I'd end up working for him because his manner of dress and lifestyle made me think he couldn't afford me," Doolen would later write. Between 1952 and 1956, Bankers Life and Casualty had spectacular growth. According to Doolen, "MacArthur was in his prime and in full control of every phase of the company."

With John in "full control," any business day could be full of surprises, and sometimes millions of dollars worth of property would be bought with the money in "petty cash." One day Lahane and Doolen picked up John at his suburban country home to go to a lawyer's office to finish a deal to acquire another insurance company. John insisted they make the rest of the trip in a decrepit, old Ford truck. How are you going to pay for the company, they asked? Wait and see, said John. At the lawyer's office, John pulled out several million dollars—in cash. The truck, they then realized, was a prop to add a bizarre, dramatic touch to the proceedings.

To stage these little jokes required being able to lay your hands on that kind of cash. It was handy that John had bought his own bank, Citizens Bank and Trust Company, of Park Ridge, Illinois, in 1955. Once an immigrant janitor, not knowing who he was (and probably knowing minimal English), wouldn't let MacArthur in the bank after closing hours. Upon learning whom he had turned away, the man feared he would be fired. MacArthur reassured him. You were just doing your job, he said. You did what you should have done.

In about 1960, another power player—attorney William Kirby— was brought onto the MacArthur team. Though Kirby and Doolen were friends, it was Kirby's success in a high-profile case before the Illinois Supreme Court—a case with issues germane to a lawsuit that John was currently facing—that brought him to Bankers' attention. John and his brother Telfer had been partners in several printing and publishing operations. One company, for instance, printed the millions of Bankers policy forms. When Telfer died, his ex-wife was unhappy with John's exercise of options to buy Telfer's stock. Lawsuits followed. It would be cheaper to hire Kirby than to bring another lawyer up to speed on the particular issues (overlapping board members) involved, advised John's legal department. Later Kirby would become general counsel for Bankers, plus MacArthur's personal attorney.

With a WATS line as a friendly tether, John was letting these executives and others up in Chicago make many of the day-to-day decisions about the insurance companies. But he was still keeping his hand in. Take the Saturday in late 1958, when he was driving down a Florida highway, going 80 miles per hour in a 65-mph zone. A Florida Highway Patrol officer pulled him over and wrote out a ticket to John (and listed his occupation as "president"). After paying the required small cash appearance bond, John then went to work. He not only sold Trooper James H. Raker an insurance policy, but made a note that Raker should be recruited as an insurance salesman. "Would make a good man" was written in pencil on the bottom of the appearance bond receipt.

IN MARCH 1959, John MacArthur filed a notice of intention to apply to the Florida State Legislature for creation of a new municipality. It would be the Florida city with which MacArthur would always be most strongly connected. The new town would be west of I-95 and could eventually cover 4,000 acres. It was to be called Palm Beach City, said MacArthur, who told reporters, "This will be my last development; in fact, I might sell off some of this land later."

Whoa, that name is way too confusing, said West Palm Beach, the city of some 55,000 people ten miles to the south. Besides, we might want to change *our* name to just Palm Beach City sometime in the future. "I'm no pirate," said MacArthur, who claimed he wanted to live "harmoniously" in the area. "City" became "Gardens" and the town of Palm Beach Gardens was chartered by the state legislature on June 20, 1959.

The new name fit MacArthur's plan to build a "garden city" with flowering planters on corners and winding streets named for flowers and trees. But first the land, swampy in some areas, had to be drained. It was a typically colorful MacArthur project. The city council suggested buying sea cows (or manatees) from the Miami Seaquarium to eat the water hyacinths in the canals. (The deal fell through.)

A giant, eighty-year-old banyan tree was moved to the Northlake Boulevard entrance of Palm Beach Gardens from its location in Lake Park, where a homeowner was going to have to cut it down. In a Keystone Cops scenario, the sixty-foot-tall, seventy-five-ton tree hoisted onto cargo trailers ended up crushing an earthmover, snapping power lines, and halting afternoon trains before reaching the hole dug for it in its new home. MacArthur tossed in the first shovelful of dirt. When a local minister asked what blessing he should say over the transplanted behemoth, MacArthur said that it wouldn't hurt to ask God for a little rain.

MacArthur was delighted with the tree and the publicity. *Life* magazine even carried a picture of the operation. Over the next few years, he rescued and transplanted more banyan trees. In one particularly spectacular operation, when a church in West Palm Beach decided to build a parking lot, four huge trees were loaded onto two barges and floated serenely ten miles up Lake Worth to a new home at a Palm Beach Gardens shopping center that was under construction. Banyan trees even made it into one of the quadrants of the official Palm Beach Gardens city shield. In the other three quadrants were the blue-and-green MacArthur plaid, a palm tree, and a happy family (Mom and Dad holding hands) standing in front of a flowering hibiscus hedge.

But man cannot live by hibiscus and banyan trees alone. MacArthur knew the happy families he envisioned buying houses in his happy town would need jobs. Pratt & Whitney already had a plant in the area. In the summer of 1960, RCA announced plans for a $4 million electronic data-processing plant in Palm Beach Gardens that would employ 1,000 workers to start.

Various theories were floated about the success of this economic development coup: MacArthur and RCA's David Sarnoff were friends, MacArthur was an RCA stockholder, and Bankers Life was a potentially big customer for RCA computers. All of these factors probably had bearing on RCA's decision. It didn't hurt that Palm Beach Gardens was served by a railroad and that MacArthur promised to build a million-gallon water plant that would reduce RCA's insurance rates. (In 1961, when MacArthur was named one of eight winners of the annual Horatio Alger awards, Sarnoff, a 1951 winner, would hand out the bronze desk plaques.)

With MacArthur leading the charge, schools were constructed, churches were built, and the people came. The 1970 census would name Palm Beach Gardens, which had gone from a population of one to 6,103 in a decade, the fastest-growing city in the United States. MacArthur even put up the money to "buy" an exit/entrance to the new turnpike for Palm Beach Gardens.

But not everything went smoothly between MacArthur and his fledgling town. Take the problem of bonds for the new hospital. For the first five years of the town's life, MacArthur was permitted by the state legislature to name the five members of the city council (all of them Bankers Life employees, a couple of whom often commuted from

Chicago for council meetings). Afterward, an elected board would be phased in. To build a new hospital, MacArthur put up money (which was combined with federal Hill-Burton funds). The city was to issue bonds to pay back MacArthur, but the new elected city council decided that the town had other pressing financial obligations and refused to issue the bonds. Suits and countersuits followed (they were dealing with MacArthur, after all) and in 1968 the hospital was sold to a for-profit hospital company.

Palm Beach Gardens also had municipal problems ranging from mundane to grandiose. Ongoing problems with an inadequate sewage treatment plant resulted in a moratorium on new construction until a new plant was built in 1975. Ambitious plans for a "giant" marina to rival Fort Lauderdale's, which was to be built on oceanfront property the town bought from Bankers Life ($5 million at five percent interest over fifteen years), gurgled and sank when the town's tax base couldn't keep up with payments.

But John MacArthur's town survived its early growing pains—and its founder. At the time of the town's twentieth anniversary, a local newspaper would write that Palm Beach Gardens, population 15,000, "will forever remain as his [MacArthur's] major and best-known real estate monument." Of course, like all MacArthur projects, the original idea had been to make money and produce a good return on investment for Bankers Life.

Probably there was something more at work here, mused writer Stewart Alsop in his 1965 article, "America's New Big Rich." The half-dozen men he profiled, "once they made their basic fortune, have spread the risk by diversifying, mostly into real estate. One suspects that in almost every case there is an emotional as well as financial gratification in real estate."

As MacArthur told Alsop, "You see something coming out of the ground. You see houses and bicycles and kids, where there was nothing but palmettos and rattlesnakes—that gives you more of a thrill than anything else."

CHAPTER 14

HOGS GET SLAUGHTERED

MEANWHILE, JOHN MACARTHUR continued to scoop up real estate elsewhere, popping New York office towers—the Gulf and Western Building on Columbus Circle, the Graybar Building next to Grand Central Station—into his portfolio like a shrewd King Kong.

In the early 1960s, his path happened to cross that of a tough, short, slightly rotund New York real estate broker named Louis Feil, and another important player was added to the MacArthur moneymaking juggernaut. Louie Feil was an investor in a company called Southern Realty and Utilities, a publicly traded company on the American Stock Exchange, primarily a Florida land-development company. MacArthur owned Royal American Industries, a similar type of company.

Feil suggested to MacArthur that Royal American acquire Southern. MacArthur wasn't really interested in taking over Southern, but he was impressed with the forty-seven-year-old Feil. He finally agreed to buy the company, but only if Feil stuck around to work everything out. The deal was announced in May 1962. Feil became a Bankers Life vice president, but his base of operations would always be New York.

Feil and his assistant, a young lawyer named Marty Bernstein, were soon traveling back and forth to Florida and elsewhere around the country, looking at land, helping sell past acquisitions such as the Colorado ranch land, and checking on potential investments for MacArthur and his web of companies. Until close to the end of his life, nearly every morning at about 5:00 or 5:30 A.M., MacArthur would start his day with a cup of coffee and a telephone conference with Feil: What looked good? How was this or that deal going? Who was in trouble and might need a loan?

But just as John was known, on occasion, to use a do-it-yourself lawyer kit and represent himself, he sometimes also liked to make his own real estate deals—which he wouldn't tell Feil and Bernstein about. Land for the Frenchman's Creek development in Palm Beach County was overpriced, for instance, advised his New York real estate experts. But John went ahead. "It was his money. He could do whatever he wanted with it," Bernstein would say later.

MacArthur also continued to be advised on many of his Florida land deals by a Florida real estate broker named Jerome Kelly. Kelly found out early on that dealing with MacArthur would be different from dealing with other businessmen. One day in the 1950s Jerry Kelly, who previously had been working with a Bankers vice president, got a call from MacArthur inviting him to a meeting at a little house MacArthur had just bought in Lake Park, at the corner of Evergreen and Third streets. After introducing Kelly to the others present and after a bit of business conversation, MacArthur, who sometimes got twitchy if he had to sit still too long, asked Kelly if he could swim. Outfitted with a pair of Rod's swim trunks, Kelly joined MacArthur in the pool where they swam sidestroke so they could continue to talk about Florida real estate.

Kelly became a good friend. As he continued to work for MacArthur, Kelly, whom MacArthur called "Irish," often heard the colorful aphorisms that expressed MacArthur's business philosophy. There was, for instance, "Pigs get fat and hogs get slaughtered," meaning, don't be too greedy: a good deal must be a good deal for both sides.

Kelly was sometimes on hand during Florida meetings between MacArthur and the colorful New York real estate impresario William Zeckendorf. Flamboyant and shrewd was how Zeckendorf would publicly characterize MacArthur in his autobiography. The same words were often used to describe Bill Zeckendorf himself, the larger-than-life promoter who put together the site for the United Nations headquarters, as well as many other development deals in Manhattan and elsewhere.

Both men were early risers. Both men spent much of the day with a telephone glued to their ear. But their personal styles were different. In his glory years, Zeckendorf operated from a breathtaking, I. M. Pei–designed teakwood office atop the Webb & Knapp building on Madison Avenue. MacArthur upgraded his Florida office from the corner of a rundown warehouse to a three-foot-square table in a coffee shop. Zeckendorf borrowed money. MacArthur lent money. "I'm not a builder, I'm a savior," MacArthur would say. "When someone gets caught in a wringer, they call me to get out."

Frequently, Zeckendorf was on the phone to John MacArthur, trying to sell him on a new, great investment opportunity. ("I have never been afraid of debt, because debt is what gives you leverage," claimed Zeckendorf.) When MacArthur would come to New York, Zeckendorf would put him up at his Manhattan Hotel, which was obviously pleasing to a miserly traveler like MacArthur. Probably his most unusual attempt to curry favor was his gift to MacArthur of a handsome Weimaraner puppy. MacArthur promptly named the dog Zeckendorf, "because he has a long nose." Though the dog went on to win prizes, Zeckendorf's company, Webb & Knapp, would collapse in spectacular fashion in mid-1965. "He paid me off 100 percent on the dollar," MacArthur said later. MacArthur liked "Big Bill," a man with "great imagination and zest for living," who just got "too deeply involved."

STILL, MUCH OF John MacArthur's real estate attention remained focused on Florida, and especially Palm Beach Gardens. In the late 1950s, as he assessed his young and still-scrawny town and the empty land surrounding it, he had an epiphany. Walt Disney, he heard, was looking for a place to locate an East Coast version of his successful California Disneyland. *Why not Palm Beach Gardens?* According to one version of the story, MacArthur, Disney, and RCA each contributed $100,000 for a feasibility study.

It was obvious what Disney and MacArthur would get out of the deal. But why was RCA involved? RCA not only was putting a new plant in the area, but it was the parent company of the NBC television network. RCA would join with MacArthur to help finance the new Disney World, and in exchange Disney would switch its popular TV program from ABC to NBC.

Walt Disney slipped quietly into Palm Beach Gardens to discuss the deal in person with RCA officials and MacArthur. Disney and MacArthur apparently hit it off just fine. There were stories that MacArthur even took Disney skinny-dipping at the half-mile stretch of pristine beach he now owned on the north end of Singer Island. Air Force Beach, as it was commonly known, had been popular with servicemen stationed during World War II at the nearby air base in West Palm Beach, as well as with area nudists.

Disney and MacArthur shook hands on the deal. To MacArthur, a deal sealed with a handshake was more than just pressing the flesh. At a later meeting, however, the whole thing unraveled, according to Jerry Kelly, who was at the meeting. The Disney organization was represented this time not by Walt but by Roy Disney, Walt's older brother, who handled the financial side of the magic kingdoms. The earlier agreement gave Disney 320 acres along Monet Road (later PGA Boulevard). But now, regardless of the earlier handshake deal, Roy wanted more land.

Earlier, in California, Disney had only been able to afford 270 acres for Disneyland. Disney had lost income when other business interests snuggled up to the edges of Disneyland, making their own profits from souvenirs, food, and lodging, and creating what some would later call "a neon jungle." Not this time, said Roy.

Shortly thereafter at lunchtime, MacArthur said he was leaving. Kelly was amazed and pulled MacArthur aside. "I have to get the hell out of here or I'll hit that goddamn beagle right in the nose," said MacArthur to Kelly. In November 1965, the Disney organization announced that its new Florida theme park would be built outside Orlando.

A mellower MacArthur, reminiscing in a later interview, said, "The Disney project for Palm Beach Gardens died a natural death." Disney had made enough money building exhibits for the 1964 World's Fair and on other projects that it didn't need his money, said MacArthur. By then (1974), MacArthur possibly had come to realize that the amount of land (27,500 acres) that Disney had eventually purchased outside Orlando would have made Disney World impractical for Palm Beach Gardens.

O.K. NO DISNEY theme park, but MacArthur had other ideas for bringing entertainment and publicity to his new town. The schemes were eclectic, to say the least, ranging from Billy Graham to the filming of the television show *Gentle Ben*. Billy Graham, who had known MacArthur's preacher-father so many years earlier, was contacted about building Billy Graham University in Palm Beach Gardens. He declined, according to MacArthur, because he felt he was primarily a preacher, not an educator, and didn't want to spread himself too thin.

Another MacArthur idea was to get publicity for the opening of the town's first church by making it a "shrine" to motherhood and to Anna Jarvis, the founder of the Mother's Day holiday in the early 1900s. His promotional director was excited. There would be chimes, a perpetual gas flame, and participation by florists and greeting-card companies. There was one hitch—convincing Philadelphia to give up the body of Jarvis so that she could be reburied in Palm Beach Gardens. Absolutely not, said a highly agitated Philadelphia. Probably just as well, since a reburied Anna Jarvis would not have rested easy as part of MacArthur's promotion scheme. She didn't even like using the holiday to sell flowers and greeting cards, which she called "a poor excuse for the letter you are too lazy to write."

One idea did take hold, and it involved snatching not a dead body, but the headquarters of a sports organization, the Professional Golfers' Association. John MacArthur didn't know a divot from a driver, but he did know Lou Strong, president of the PGA. With promises of land for a new clubhouse and two championship golf courses, MacArthur lured the organization from Dunedin on Florida's west coast across the state to Palm Beach Gardens. And when the organization couldn't raise the money for its elegant new clubhouse, MacArthur lent them $1.5 million. There was a lawsuit, of course, between MacArthur and a new organization board, but MacArthur ended up renting the whole shebang to the PGA for $40,000 a year, with reduced rates for association members.

But the Palm Beach Gardens duffers were not forgotten. Eventually MacArthur would build a third eighteen-hole course for the locals who complained that they couldn't play when PGA events were in town.

CHAPTER 15
THE COLONNADES

SINGER ISLAND—technically a peninsula—is one of South Florida's barrier islands. At the north end of Palm Beach County, it had once been connected by a narrow spit of land to Palm Beach, the island to the south. From 1918 on, a dredged inlet from the Atlantic Ocean to Lake Worth separated the two islands, just as residents' different lifestyles would later do the same.

In 1963, John MacArthur made one of his most significant real estate purchases. He bought the fifteen-year-old Colonnades Beach Hotel, a hodgepodge of low white buildings at the south end of Singer Island. It was a significant purchase not just because of the profits it would produce, but because, as it turned out, it gave him a grand, if slightly down-at-the-heels stage on which to live out the rest of his life. The sixty-six-year-old MacArthur increasingly seemed to like to have an audience for his wisecracks and eccentricities.

Singer Island got its name in the 1920s because of a wealthy European named Paris Singer, heir to the Singer sewing machine fortune and, for a time, a Palm Beach resident. Singer, whose colorful past included a six-year liaison with modern dance pioneer Isadora Duncan (he was the father of one of her sons), would bring his Palm Beach friends by boat to the island for picnics. Here they found pristine, gorgeous beaches, where gentle Atlantic swells rolled in, then tumbled back out into an ocean of turquoise, then sapphire, then deep midnight blue. Singer envisioned building two hotels on the island, but those ambitious plans were halted by the 1928 hurricane and the 1929 stock market crash. Singer died in London in 1932. The derelict skeleton of the beginnings of the

Blue Heron, his hotel at the north end of "Singer's Island," was finally torn down and sold as scrap metal in the early years of World War II.

The next Englishman to see the possibilities of Singer Island was A. O. Edwards, whose earlier construction projects included the Savoy, Mayfair, and Grosvenor House hotels in London. After crossing a rickety wooden bridge to visit the island in 1947, Edwards, now an American citizen and winter resident of Palm Beach, embarked on an energetic plan to develop the south end of Singer Island. His new community of Palm Beach Shores offered "people of modest means" Florida sunshine (FHA financing available) and "a simple outdoor life the year 'round, with gentle trade winds blowing cool in summer and warm in winter." (The Gulf Stream was said to flow closer to Singer Island than any other spot along the Florida coast.)

In early 1949, partially to accommodate potential lot buyers checking out the area, Edwards opened a new hotel on the ocean side of Palm Beach Shores called the Inlet Court Hotel. But Inlet Court projected the wrong image. It sounded too much like "tourist court," as early motels were often called. Edwards changed the name to the Colonnades. The new name came from the arched, vaguely Arabic, cloistered porches that connected and ran along the sides of the buildings, scooping up trade wind breezes. Just how unchic the hotel was, however, is indicated by the fact that it was the only hotel in this winter-playground–area to stay open all year-round.

Edwards died in 1960. MacArthur bought the hotel from the estate several years later for $650,000, despite advice from visiting Bill Zeckendorf that he ought to tear down the old wreck. "This is nothing but a fleabag," Zeckendorf told him. "I wouldn't touch it with a ten-foot pole."

Where others saw fleas, MacArthur saw potential raffish charm. He had found a starved, mistreated dog by the side of the road and, against all contrary advice, was determined to save it. "Suppose I had torn it down and built a new hotel," MacArthur would tell Miami newspaper columnist Nixon Smiley a few years later as remodeling progressed. "What would I have? Nothing but a goddamn box, like they've got at

Miami Beach. Now I'm getting something with character; something distinctive." (Smiley toured Florida looking for interesting characters and places for his *Miami Herald* column, and with MacArthur he hit pay dirt. He became a frequent visitor.)

MacArthur raised the roof—literally—adding another floor and more guest rooms, including twenty duplex apartments, adding new restaurants, and expanding the first-floor banquet facility. By the time he was done remodeling the Colonnades (in about 1968) it would have 400 rooms, four floors in some sections, and little remaining of its original, pre-MacArthur self, except the arched colonnades. As with most MacArthur projects, there were complaints and suits and injunctions— for construction noise, accumulated trash, and allegedly dumping of sewage into the ocean. Eventually, John and Catherine would move into one of those duplex apartments, and John would famously set up shop each day at an ordinary small square table in the coffee shop— telephone(s) ready, coffee cup full, ashtray overflowing. From here, he could keep an eye on things as he closed real estate deals, checked in with the Chicago office, even talked to reporters. "If I took these guys [businessmen, developers] up to my office, I'd have to be courteous to them," he told a visiting *New York Times* reporter. "Here I just get up and walk into the kitchen and hide."

A new, glossy brochure for the "Colonnades Beach Hotel" carried what was a version of a MacArthur clan crest, including the motto "Fide et Opera"—Fidelity and Labor. (John had his own saltier translation of the Latin.) The brochure described seven tennis courts, two swimming pools, deep-sea fishing, nearby golf, a quarter-mile beach, and 250 rooms "set amidst sixteen acres of lushly landscaped private grounds." Because there were, as yet, no other big hotels in northern Palm Beach County, the Colonnades was where the local action was, the place for community meetings, luncheons, and teen dances. As a later ad for attracting convention business put it, "We're not The Breakers and we don't try to be. But neither are our prices."

The Colonnades was particularly popular with Canadian tourists and tour groups. It was the place to catch a glimpse, occasionally, of celebrities like Jackie Gleason or Bob Hope or Burt Reynolds having lunch with Dinah Shore. (Burt's father had worked for John.) It was, of course, good publicity for the hotel when celebrities stayed at the hotel. MacArthur, for instance, went to great lengths to woo Hope away from Palm Beach by preparing a special penthouse suite for the comedian that opened out onto a rooftop deck. There was nothing subtle about MacArthur-style décor. "Welcome to the BOB HOPE SUITE" was painted beneath the staircase of the two-floor suite. A large, glittery chandelier hung in the stairwell (rumor had it that it had been converted from a carved cypress parakeet cage that once hung in Miami's Roney Plaza hotel).

There were small, stained glass windows in the suite's "ladies room" and a grand piano that had belonged to either Irving Berlin, or Palm Beach architect Addison Mizner, or Palm Beach resident Robert "Believe It or Not" Ripley, according to local legend. As a gag, MacArthur once put on a waiter's jacket and, with hotel photographer in tow, answered Hope's call for room service, pouring a cup of coffee for an apparently surprised Hope. The resulting photo (with an ever-present cigarette dangling from the ersatz waiter's mouth) made the newspapers.

It was the hotel's atmosphere, not its architecture, that was memorable, remembered a MacArthur associate decades later. "It didn't have a Palm Beach address, but there was a lot of ambience. You could sit at the carousel bar and see lots of celebrities in an hour. . . . To dine at the Colonnades when the moon was climbing over the Gulf Stream, oh, that was spectacular."

Though MacArthur focused much of his attention on Florida and the Colonnades, the rest of his empire was not hanging slack. There was Las Vegas, for instance. Howard Hughes, another member of America's eccentric billionaire brotherhood, had settled in the desert town. Hughes's increasingly untethered persona made MacArthur seem apple-pie normal in comparison. The two men had done business in the past, including the buying and selling of a war-surplus airplane. Hughes owned the Desert Inn, across Las Vegas Boulevard ("the Strip") from MacArthur's Frontier Hotel.

A bright new, very large Frontier sign was installed as part of a $6 million remodeling project. Its flashing light shone into the upper floors of the Desert Inn, disturbing Hughes, who famously liked everything dark and kept heavy shades on his windows. Turn off the sign, said Hughes's people to MacArthur's people. Nuts to that, responded MacArthur. It's my hotel.

Then I'll buy your hotel, said Hughes, who was on a Las Vegas buying spree. When Hughes asked what he wanted for it, MacArthur mentioned what he thought was an outlandish price—and Hughes agreed, to MacArthur's surprise. When MacArthur and Louie Feil arrived in Las Vegas to close the deal, Hughes announced that his lawyer would be representing him, according to MacArthur's later telling of the story. "Hell, what was I going to do? I said, 'Mr. Feil will represent me,' and I left."

As indicated by his enjoyment of the publicity created by his ransom of the DeLong Ruby for the American Museum of Natural History, MacArthur was savoring the national limelight. It appeared that Fame had gotten its hooks into him. In the mid-1960s, he decided to get into the entertainment business himself—again, probably motivated by a desire to bring publicity (and business) to his Florida properties. The first project started out as part of a complex deal between MacArthur and Ivor Tors, the Hungarian-born animal trainer and film producer. The deal would have brought a movie production studio and Tors's wild animals to Palm Beach Gardens. (Some said that MacArthur was trying to out-Disney Disney and its Orlando theme park.)

After the deal with Tors fell apart, MacArthur went ahead on his own, and in 1967, a six-day-a-week game show called *Treasure Isle* premiered on ABC television. (MacArthur owned local station WEAT.) MacArthur had scooped out a "tropical lagoon" on the Colonnades lawn. With palm trees and the Atlantic Ocean as a backdrop, young couples, guided by maps and clues, would paddle about hunting for buried treasure. As it happened, Hurricane Betsy had deposited a Greek freighter, the *Amaryllis*, on the beach near the hotel a few years earlier, and shots of the wreck added authentic color to the setting. Kids in the neighborhood loved to come down and watch the show in production. The program lasted one season.

The Colonnades got more serious exposure when Rutgers University held its annual seminar for state legislators at the hotel in the mid-1960s. The program brought together about fifty of the country's outstanding state lawmakers for workshops on the reform and improvement of state legislatures. For two years, the seminar had been held at Key Biscayne. Now it had come to the Colonnades, snagged by MacArthur who was, as always, trying to build the hotel's convention business.

Among the attendees greeted by the old man sitting in the coffee shop was a young Jesse Uhru, who would one day be the high-profile leader of the California Senate, and Florida legislator Bob Graham, whose father's land north of Miami MacArthur had tried to buy so many years earlier.

What Rutgers organizers *really* hoped for, of course, was financial backing for the project from MacArthur. What they got was a welcoming address from the staunchly conservative MacArthur that at least some considered embarrassingly gauche and condescending—totally inappropriate for a bipartisan group. It was perhaps yet another example of MacArthur's tin ear—of his not being able to gauge how his words would affect the people hearing them, or of not caring. After two years, the Rutgers seminar moved on to The Breakers in Palm Beach—without money from Florida's John D.

ANOTHER VISITOR lurking about the Colonnades (as some would have it) during the 1960s was a writer named William Hoffman. In 1969 Hoffman's book, a rather scabrous, gossipy work about John MacArthur called *The Stockholder*, was published by Lyle Stuart, himself a colorful, controversial publisher who specialized in "gut topics: money, sex, health, crime," said *Forbes* magazine. In later years, Hoffman said that he lived for a month at the Colonnades. He generally didn't mention that he was a former editor of one of the Bankers Life company publications.

Lively and detailed but full of long paragraphs of fabricated, reconstructed dialogue, the book was full of heavy-breathing passages, like the one describing the young Catherine as "inordinately ambitious" with "an exquisite body which she was fully prepared to use in the furtherance of her interests." John, of course, was portrayed in all his raw, profane, suspect-business-dealing glory.

The book's title, though not exactly a marketing department's delight, did accurately convey the key to MacArthur's wealth—that he was the sole stockholder, owner, of the money machine that was Bankers Life and all the companies it had gobbled up. Though writing off the book as maybe "more an act of spite than of journalism," *Business Week* admitted in its review that the writer did seem to know a lot of details about the business. It was hard for other readers to judge, since no sources (i.e., footnotes or endnotes) were given for Hoffman's information. In a later MacArthur Foundation–published history of the family, *The MacArthur Heritage*, the bibliography listed Hoffman's book as "a sensationalized version of John's life [that] should be read more as entertainment than as historical fact."

Meanwhile, up in Chicago, members of the family (particularly Alfred's branch) chortled at *The Stockholder* and wondered if perhaps John himself had written it, since some of the details only he would have known. Actually, John was livid about the book, writes another MacArthur observer on the scene, Bob Sanford, the bartender at the Colonnades. The hotel was rife with rumors that MacArthur was so upset by the book—"a pack of goddamn lies"—that he intended to buy up the copyright and see that it was never reprinted, Sanford would write in *John D. MacArthur: A View from the Bar.* "Once I read the book I guessed what the problem was—it was unauthorized, and he wasn't making any money from it!" Sanford added.

Another visitor to the hotel at the time said the book seemed to have "hurt his [MacArthur's] feelings." Publicly, MacArthur was relaxed about the whole thing. "He [Hoffman] downplayed the luck" involved in building his empire, MacArthur told a reporter.

Behind the scenes, however, executives at Bankers Life were trying to figure out how to react. They carefully monitored author Hoffman's brief appearance on the David Frost television show, where the topic was gambling as an addiction (topic of another Hoffman book), and they reported that nothing was said about Bankers or MacArthur. John's son Rod was upset and suggested another book be commissioned. John, in typically pungent style, told him to forget it. "The more you stir up an old turd, the worse it stinks." John added, in a memo to Bankers executive Paul Doolen, "I have never referred to the book in any interview other than to say the author never saw me until after the book was written."

MacArthur may or may not have been reassured by the *Chicago Tribune*'s book review, which said, "The old warrior . . . deserves better than what William Hoffman has given him. He deserves closer study, more penetrating thought. If hatchet job it must be, he deserves at least a certain deftness of stroke and a clean, well-sharpened blade."

CHAPTER 16

FOUNDING A FOUNDATION

THE OLD BLUE-and-white, twin-engine Aero Commander turned and banked over the line of palm trees and oaks, landing efficiently if not smoothly on the 3,000-foot-long airstrip that had been hacked out of the central Florida ranch land. Since this was a working cattle ranch and herds were sometimes moved along the wide, mowed grass strip, often chips of cow manure would splatter up onto the plane's windshield.

The plane thumped to a stop—even a highly skilled pilot like the former second-in-command of Cuba's pre-Castro air force could do only so much when landing on this terrain—and down climbed John MacArthur and lawyer Bill Kirby, in from Chicago. Kirby was on a mission of some urgency. Potential chaos in the MacArthur financial empire loomed if something were not done soon about the potential tax liability of the MacArthur estate.

By now even MacArthur realized, after his hospitalization a few months earlier during the winter of 1969–1970, that he wasn't going to live forever. In fact, doctors hadn't expected him to leave the hospital at all. What was originally thought to be viral pneumonia had turned very serious, with the seventy-two-year-old MacArthur drifting in and out of consciousness and finally requiring a tracheotomy. Later tests revealed stomach cancer, so part of his stomach was removed. However, MacArthur had shown 'em. Here he was, up walking around again after surgery and several months of recuperation, although his eyes were surrounded by large, smudged gray circles, dark as the undersides of the rain clouds that blew across the mid-Florida ranch most afternoons.

For MacArthur, a trip to the 10,000-acre working cattle ranch, which he had owned for about two years now, was always relaxing. He delighted in bumping in a Jeep or Ford pickup over the dusty roads to show guests the ranch's handsome herds of short-horned Angus and Herefords crossed with Brahman (to handle South Florida's heat). Or he would gleefully point out the impressive reproductive attributes of "Sugar," Buck Island Ranch's most recently purchased prize purebred bull.

Buck Island Ranch was an "island" only in a central-Florida sense. Bordering the ranch on the west and south was the Harney Pond Canal, fed by Buck Creek and running east, eventually, to Lake Okeechobee. It was part of the network of flood control canals that helped the state's farmers irrigate during the dry season and drain fields during the rains. Often alligators could be spotted sunning alongside this canal or one of the drainage ditches that crisscrossed the ranch.

For visitors from the Midwest like Kirby, there was also not only the odd sight of cattle lounging under palm trees, but also the abundant numbers of fidgety, white tropical birds—cattle egrets—that skillfully dodged hooves as they searched for bugs stirred up by the big beasts' moving feet. Another treat for guests, if the season was right, was picking ripe grapefruit and oranges in the ranch's 160-acre grove of citrus trees.

This visit by Kirby, however, was not for relaxation or fruit picking. Kirby, as general counsel for Bankers Life and Casualty, as well as MacArthur's personal attorney, foresaw huge problems looming and a potential unraveling of one of the country's largest private financial empires unless a definite plan was made, and soon.

Ever since he had bought his first insurance company, MacArthur had controlled just about everything he touched with cunning, charm, and, if necessary, chicanery. But there would be no controlling death. When he was gone, his massive holdings would be as vulnerable as the wind-whipped floppy nests of one of the ranch's *other* endangered species, a striking two-foot-tall bird, the black-crested caracara, which lucky visitors very occasionally glimpsed.

The ranch was on the eastern edge of the narrow band in central Florida that was one of the few places of natural habitat in the United States for the big, long-legged, black-and-white bird with the distinctive orange wipe across its beak. "Buzzards" the ranch hands called them. Crested caracaras were among the miscellaneous wildlife—white-tailed deer, armadillos, sandhill cranes, wild turkeys, bobcats, the occasional panther, and, of course, alligators—that shared the ranch with the cattle when John MacArthur had purchased it in April 1968.

Only the sellers, two brothers named J. C. and Ralph Durrance, didn't know they were selling to one of the country's richest men, who was well on his way to becoming the largest individual private land-owner in Florida. They thought they were selling their ranch to a tall, affable, and knowledgeable rancher from Colorado who had been look-ing for more than a year for the right parcel of land. It had to be south of Vero Beach, subtropical land (which would have the longest frost-free period), partially unimproved with marsh and woods (for the cattle in winter), and with sweet soil, good for growing all-important clover on which fine beef cattle thrive and produce plump calves. That lanky rancher had, in fact, been working for John MacArthur for many decades, managing farm and ranch operations (as a "participating partner") for him in Nevada, Colorado, and New Mexico.

"We got a real good buy," ranch manager Dan Childs would say with a chuckle many years later. The land went for about $100 an acre— 14 percent down, with an interest on the rest of 3 percent to 4 percent. (After MacArthur's death, the ranch would be valued at $1,500 to $2,000 an acre.) For once it was not just the thrill of the chase. MacArthur loved the ranch, loved having a place close enough to his home base in Palm Beach Shores that he could fly or drive to on weekends. And with his aging Aero Commander in the hands of Felipe Catasus, the trip from Palm Beach Shores was no more trouble than stepping across the street. MacArthur had found the ex-Cuban air force pilot working as a me-

The MacArthur family in about 1901.
Left to right, front row: Telfer, John,
Charles; middle row: Georgiana,
Helen, William, Alfred; standing,
right rear: Marguerite. *Nyack College
Archives and Special Collections*

Georgiana often dressed her two
youngest boys alike—Charles (left)
and John, about 1904. *Huttar Collection,
Nyack College Archives and Special
Collections*

During World War I, John learned to fly in Canada and served as a pilot with the Royal Flying Corps. *Historical Society of Palm Beach County* After the war he returned to Oak Park, Illinois, and married Louise Ingalls. *University of Wisconsin-Madison Archives*

In 1941, John MacArthur moved a growing Bankers Life and Casualty Company into a former bank building at 4444 W. Lawrence Avenue. The insurance company headquarters would eventually sprawl throughout the near-westside Chicago neighborhood. *Bankers Life and Casualty Archives*

John and Catherine MacArthur (center) at a Bankers Life event. Paul Doolen, (second from left with Mrs. Doolen), considered by some to be John's alter ego, served at various times as vice-chairman of the Bankers board and as company president. *Bankers Life and Casualty Archives*

John, Catherine, and Charlie MacArthur at a family wedding at "Pretty Penny," the home on the Hudson River in Nyack, New York, of Helen Hayes and Charles MacArthur. The bride's mother, Helen Mac-Arthur Bishop (John and Charlie's sister), is just visible over Charlie's shoulder. *Photo by Rod MacArthur*

Florida real estate developer John MacArthur took pride in rescuing endangered trees. These four banyan trees were floated by barge up Lake Worth to a new home in Palm Beach Gardens. *State Archives of Florida*

Catherine and John MacArthur, and poodle Lulu Belle. *Nyack College Archives and Special Collections*

The screened porch of MacArthur's modest Buck Island ranch house is where attorney Bill Kirby finally convinced MacArthur to put the bulk of his estate into a foundation. Papers establishing the John D. and Catherine T. MacArthur Foundation were signed in October 1970 at MacArthur's Colonnades Hotel.

Successful playwright Charles MacArthur arrives in Chicago in 1936. *Chicago History Museum*

Actor James MacArthur and his mother, the actress Helen Hayes, were on hand in Tallahassee in 1974 when Florida State University announced plans for the Charles MacArthur Center for the American Theatre. *Claire Crawford Collection*

John D. MacArthur was "at ease," unlike some tycoons he had drawn, said artist LeRoy Neiman, who sketched the aging billionaire wearing a green family plaid jacket at an awards ceremony in 1977, just seven months before his death. *Courtesy of LeRoy Neiman*

John Roderick (Rod) MacArthur had a mercurial relationship with his father, John D., until the very end. Rod made his own fortune in limited-edition collectible plates. *The Bradford Group*

Comedian Bob Hope was a friend of MacArthur's and sometimes stayed at the Colonnades in a grandiose, two-level suite named for the entertainer. *Davidoff Studios*

A year before he died, an ailing John MacArthur left his sick bed to greet Palm Beach neighbor Rose Kennedy when she spoke at a conference at the Colonnades. *Davidoff Studios*

Always the good actress, Helen Hayes beams as she appears beside her brother-in-law at a dinner of Bankers Life's popular Bankervetts employee organization. *Bankers Life and Casualty Archives*

chanic in a repair shop near John's small private airfield near Singer Island. Catasus's gratitude was so great for getting a job where he could fly again that he would never leave the house if he thought MacArthur might call—to the distress of his wife, who sometimes had other plans for weekend outings.

A TEN-MINUTE ride from the ranch airstrip at Buck Island was the modest, one-story ranch house constructed of vertical California redwood boards and painted deep red, which the property's previous owners had built as a weekend place. Now it was the full-time home of ranch manager Dan Childs and his wife, Anita. The house had been built with a large central room with broad fireplace, flanked on either end by a set of two bedrooms and a bathroom—one side for each of the two Durrance brothers.

These days the bedrooms on the south were used by Dan and Anita Childs (their two children were grown). The bedrooms at the other end were used by John MacArthur when he visited and weekend houseguests. Sometimes the weekend guests included John's latest lady friend. John still liked the ladies; Catherine seldom came to the ranch. ("These days, patting an ass is just like squeezing a hand used to be," MacArthur would tell a reporter a few years later. "I've never had an affair worthy of the name, though I have snuck around a little, as any man would admit he's done, if he's honest.")

Sometimes there were guests like actor Burt Reynolds, who mostly lounged around watching football on TV when he and MacArthur were not talking about a possible movie about Florida, which MacArthur might finance.

At Buck Island, Anita, who had been cooking for ranch hands most of her life, would generally cook for John and any guests in the kitchen and eating area at one end of the large central room. And at least once, when the power went out, she and John did the cooking over the room's open fireplace. (Their ideas on kitchen management differed, however. John had been known to take "perfectly good" food out of the trash after Anita had cleaned out the refrigerator.)

If there were large groups visiting, such as the local cattlemen's organization, Dan Childs would fire up the smoker or big pit barbeque that he had built behind the house in the grove of pines and palms (or "hammock," as folks around here called such a stand of trees). One of the best features of the ranch house was a long screened porch on the back of the house that stretched between the bedroom wings and overlooked the verdant hammock. It was here that Kirby and MacArthur settled into rocking chairs and continued their discussions of what would happen to MacArthur's fortune after he was gone.

Too much sitting, however, made MacArthur restless. From time to time, during business conversations, John would pull his startled guests out of their rocking chairs. "Come on," he would tell them, "we're going to earn an honest dollar." He would grab a couple of hoes, jump into one of the ranch trucks, and have Dan Childs or someone drive poor Kirby (or whoever was visiting) out to chop thistles in one of the fields. Such dirt-under-the-fingernails moments never lasted too long, however, because MacArthur's lifetime of smoking (he chain-smoked cheap Domino cigarettes or Winstons) had seriously reduced his physical stamina.

Back at the ranch house, Kirby and MacArthur rocked and talked. For several years MacArthur had balked at even considering the matter of the disposition of his fortune. "I'm a better salesman than you are, and I could never get people to talk about death, and you are not going to be able to get me to talk about death," the old pro told his lawyer. "Any insurance salesman knows how hard it is to get people to talk about death. Instead, you talk about money for their old age or protection for education for their children. I don't need money for my old age," said MacArthur in the version of the events that Kirby would tell over and over again in later years, "and I am not worried about my children."

His current will, leaving half of his fortune to Catherine and half to his children, Rod and Virginia, was a disaster from a tax and estate planning perspective, Kirby had been telling MacArthur. The federal government would take most of it in taxes. Kirby knew his man. Those were red-flag words: *taxes, government.* This money is going to the public or for the public good one way or another, said Kirby. So who do you want to make the decisions on how it will be spent—"bureaucrats or people you trust?"

The whopping tax bill would mean that the "insurance family" that MacArthur had put together would have to be dismantled and disposed of at fire-sale prices to raise cash. (A reporter some years later would write that, when talking about the foundation, MacArthur seemed more motivated "out of a desire to keep his business together than any charitable purpose.") Kirby's frequent arguments about the importance of setting up a trust or foundation at last were beginning to sink in. As he headed back to Chicago after this trip, Kirby left behind the draft of possible foundation articles of incorporation for John to look over and think about.

In October 1970, Kirby flew back down to Florida. John was entertaining winners of a Bankers Life sales conference and their wives at the Colonnades for a long weekend, so it was not until Sunday morning breakfast in the coffee shop that Kirby finally got to talk to MacArthur about the legal matters that concerned him. It was important that the IRS approve the new foundation—in writing—as an appropriate charitable entity as soon as possible. And sensing the historical moment, Kirby insisted that it should be John MacArthur himself, not someone from a law firm, who signed the twenty-dollar check to the Illinois Secretary of State for the filing of the foundation incorporation papers.

The two men went upstairs to the MacArthurs' apartment where Catherine was ready to type out a check. Catherine pulled her copy of Kirby's previously prepared incorporation documents from her files. After taking a look at the words "John D. MacArthur Foundation" on the document, John said, "Put Catherine's name in there; she helped build it up." Without saying anything, she took the papers, went to her typewriter, made an erasure, and typed "John D. and Catherine T. MacArthur Foundation" onto the articles of incorporation. It may have been John's finest hour, a note of grace to their complex, often stormy, but ultimately surviving personal and business relationship.

To finish the process, three incorporators were needed, and John chose himself, Catherine, and Paul Doolen. The seven directors would be John, Catherine, Doolen, Kirby, Louie Feil, broadcaster Paul Harvey, and, after some discussion, Rod. Catherine typed in the names and Doolen and Rod MacArthur, who were both at the hotel, came up to the apartment and, taking turns at the kitchen table, signed the documents. Though the signings took place on Sunday, October 18, 1970, Kirby later noticed that the notary public, to whom Catherine had taken the papers, had dated them Monday, October 19. He surmised that perhaps the notary was suspicious that doing anything on a Sunday was illegal.

What would be the new foundation's mission? John had made it clear in the past that he didn't want to get involved in these decisions. "I'm going to do what I do best; I'm going to make it [money]. You guys will have to figure out after I am dead what to do with it," said John, according to Kirby. The language of the charter describing the purposes of the foundation was kept simple, with much of the wording taken straight from the IRS code: that the foundation would operate for "charitable, religious, scientific, literary, and educational purposes. . ."

There were, however, three illustrations of what programs might be set up ("not in limitation" of other programs). The foundation might support "ways to discover and promulgate avoidance of waste in governmental expenditures; [and] look into the problems of 'retired persons generally.'" And, thirdly, it might stipulate "that all of the foundation's operations could be undertaken either directly or by contributions to other qualified charitable organizations." The first two examples, at least, seemed close to the thrifty Scottish soul of MacArthur, who hated all kinds of extravagance and obviously was in no hurry to retire from work himself.

CHAPTER 17

PALM BEACH PROMETHEUS

ON THE LAST Sunday in February 1971, Jack Nicklaus, his blond hair rumpled by the light breeze, sank a short put and walked off the eighteenth hole of the PGA golf course in Palm Beach Gardens with a new record. By winning the PGA for a second time, the thirty-one-year-old Nicklaus had become the first player ever to win all four of the world's major tournaments at least twice (the others: the Masters, the British Open, and the U.S. Open).

On hand for his victory were his wife, celebrating a birthday, and nine-year-old son, Jackie. "I feel great," said Nicklaus, now practically a John MacArthur neighbor since he had moved to Lost Tree Village, a few miles up the coast in North Palm Beach.

John MacArthur had been holding court off and on all week, greeting players, talking to reporters, and sizing up the crowds from the balcony of the sumptuous PGA clubhouse. But behind the scenes all was not well. Soon rumors began to surface that the PGA was pulling its headquarters out of Palm Beach Gardens and moving to Pinehurst, North Carolina, before its lease expired at the end of 1974.

Off the fairways, disagreements had been festering for some time. Among MacArthur's complaints: PGA annual meetings were not being held at the Colonnades as he had expected. Other sites (in Michigan and Ohio) had been chosen for the 1972 and 1973 PGA National Championships, though MacArthur had hoped to make this powerhouse tournament an annual event in Palm Beach Gardens.

MacArthur decided to strike first. Shortly before the PGA's November 1972 annual meeting (in Los Angeles), MacArthur held a press conference to announce that he was kicking the PGA out of its Palm Beach Gardens headquarters at the end of the year, even though the lease had two more years to run. "You are now and always have been in violation of your agreement that I was induced to enter to save the PGA," MacArthur grouched in a letter to the organization's president. MacArthur, who had claimed at a public ceremony six months earlier that he didn't "run the bases" like he used to, nevertheless was obviously still in fighting fettle.

Meanwhile, another MacArthur grand deal was coming unstitched, but this one, at least, was due to forces beyond MacArthur's control. RCA announced in 1971 that it would close its Palm Beach Gardens plant. It was all part of greater problems at RCA. The company's electronic data-processing sector had become "a shambles" and "a debacle," business historian Robert Sobel would later write.

But there were always other deals waiting in the wings for someone with ready cash in his pocket. Two MacArthur hotel acquisitions in the early 1970s within a few miles of one another demonstrated the extremes of MacArthur real estate deals—and taste. At one end of the spectrum was the shabby, old Sea Spray Motel next door to the Colonnades. Its purchase let the Colonnades expand north along the Singer Island beach, giving MacArthur about 1,700 feet total of prized ocean frontage. At the other extreme was the famous, old doddering dowager, the Biltmore Hotel in Palm Beach, a beauty in her day but now forced to close and threatened by demolition.

MacArthur said he had once stayed at the Biltmore and had fallen in love with the place (a surprisingly uncharacteristic emotion for MacArthur to show toward real estate). Built in 1926 and originally named the Alba, the large, Spanish-style building on the Lake Worth side of posh Palm Beach soon became the playground of visiting movie stars and European royalty. It was said that floodlights shining on the Biltmore's ornate, twin towers signaled that the Palm Beach ten-week "season" had begun. But times and fashion change. Eventually the hotel passed into the hands of the Teamsters Union Pension Fund, from whom

MacArthur bought it for $1.5 million. It would not be torn down, he announced, though his exact plans for the structure were on hold while he recuperated from recent health problems.

JOHN MACARTHUR thought of himself as a conservationist. Hadn't he rescued all those banyan trees? Ridden on the front of a bulldozer to save more trees when Palm Beach Gardens and the PGA golf course were laid out?

What a shock, then, to realize that landmark environmental legislation passed by the 1972 Florida legislature was aimed at saving Florida from people like him: developers who dredged where they wanted, built what they wanted, without so much as a by-your-leave of any blankety-blank land-use planning authority. A new environmental consciousness was walking the halls of Florida's historic old capitol building in Tallahassee. Florida's unfettered real estate development was at last being reined in.

Fresh, sweet water had always been one of Florida's blessings. Early naturalists had marveled at the clarity of the lakes, rivers, and springs, so clear that "one could watch a tiny button sink slowly to the bottom," Nelson Manfred Blake would write a few years later in his landmark book *Land Into Water—Water Into Land.* But decades of man's remodeling—canals draining the Everglades and other swampy areas, agricultural runoff, unending increases in population—were having repercussions. Some said it was an increase in such headline-grabbing events as cars suddenly dropping into sink holes (admittedly still rare) that showed that Florida's underground water reservoirs were in trouble and got the public's attention—and that of its representatives.

The four key bills passed by the 1972 legislature dealt with controlling, conserving, and managing water; establishing comprehensive state planning of growth; and state purchase of environmentally endangered lands. Citizens of Boca Raton, south of West Palm Beach, voted to put a cap on the number of living units in the town. "Promethean man could sometime improve on nature, but painful experience was teaching him humility," wrote Blake.

Palm Beach County's Prometheus was neither humble nor happy. "You need a permit for everything," fumed MacArthur. "Not one permit, but nine of them for everything. You can't dig a hole without a permit from somebody." Some saw John MacArthur as a throwback to the crusty, independent Florida old-timers—the "Crackers," the Marjorie Kinnan Rawlings characters who did what they pleased, ignoring the authorities and their wimpy laws.

In early April 1973, John MacArthur held a press conference and announced that he was going to begin getting rid of his Florida holdings "in an orderly fashion," starting with the sale of his West Palm Beach TV station. He gave his age as the main reason. "I'm thirty days into my seventy-seventh year. I feel a lot of these things have to be settled while the old man's still around," he told one of the local newspapers. MacArthur was currently charged with a misdemeanor violation of state dredge-and-fill laws, and several groups were opposing his plans to develop Big Munyon Island in the Intracoastal Waterway between Singer Island and the mainland. The battles continued, but the fun was gone.

"I don't like some smart aleck that doesn't own a twenty-five-foot lot telling me to build one house on five acres or not to build at all because it will ruin the beauty of the wilderness," he said a few weeks later. "I believe in zoning and respect for my neighbors, but the pendulum has swung too far. Florida is so bad because it has so many retirees running around with nothing to do but gang up on the legislators," he added.

But, he insisted, he wasn't mad at Florida and had no intention of surrendering his "Florida passport."

CHAPTER 18

LOST AND SOMETIMES FOUND

ACTUALLY, JOHN MACARTHUR was rather pleased with what was going on elsewhere in Florida. In February 1972, Florida State University in Tallahassee had inaugurated the school's new American Playwright Series by staging a performance of the Charles MacArthur/Ben Hecht comedy *Twentieth Century*, first presented on Broadway in 1932. On hand in Tallahassee for the celebratory weekend were John, Helen Hayes, and James MacArthur, Charles and Helen's son. The young actor sported sideburns and a hit television show *Hawaii Five-O*, at the time in its fifth season.

The gala day was the result of a theatrical friendship between Richard Fallon, founder of the university's theater department, and Helen Hayes. As a young actor, Fallon had auditioned for a part in the 1946–1947 Broadway play *Happy Birthday*, by playwright Anita Loos, in which Hayes was to star. Fallon didn't get the part, but the handsome young actor with the resonant voice did impress Helen Hayes, and a long friendship resulted. It continued even after Fallon moved from acting into teaching theater at the university level.

At the Florida State luncheon preceding the evening performance, the university's president spoke, Florida Senate resolution number 1138 was read, and a plaque was presented to the family. Charles MacArthur was honored for his "contribution to the theater in developing a genre of American comedy [that] established him as one of America's leading playwrights."

As it turned out, not all of the weekend's acting was on the stage. The relationship between Helen and John was at times mercurial (like

John's relationships with many people). Though the two posed together throughout the weekend—Helen beaming, her famous face tilted characteristically to the side, John slicked up with jacket and tie—her remarks about her brother-in-law in a letter to a reporter at about the same time were less sanguine. "He invited me once to go to Florida and live in some development he was promoting," she wrote to a Florida reporter who was preparing a wire-service profile on "America's Least Known Billionaire."

"I knew if I did," she continued, "John would have me riding through the streets naked on a white horse to get some publicity for it, so I didn't go. As far as his providing for me [financially], he never did a thing. It was his brother, my beloved Alfred, who did that. With John, it's been the other way around. I guess I've given him more [presents] than he has ever given me." The United Press International story appeared in papers around the country, with the reporter's parenthetical comment that Alfred MacArthur had died leaving "a mere $300 million." Yet all appeared to be reasonably amicable two years later when Helen, John, and James were again on hand at FSU to honor Charlie.

It seemed that a doctoral student, who had spent a year at Florida State, was writing a dissertation on "Character Delineation in the Stage Plays of Charles MacArthur." John Irvine had found an unprocessed collection of material about the playwright at another university, which agreed to send him copies. In going through the copies, Irvine discovered the script for a "lost" MacArthur play, *Stag at Bay*. Written with Nunnally Johnson in the late 1930s, the play was based on a story MacArthur told about his pal, John Barrymore. The play was finished in about 1951 but never given a full production. Irvine told Fallon, who notified his friend Helen. Fallon offered to produce the play at FSU. The actress was delighted.

In February 1974, *Stag at Bay* at last had its world premiere, with a professional director and two professional actors hired for the leads. Another part of the premiere weekend was the publication of the book *The Stage Works of Charles MacArthur*, with forewords by both Helen and

John and an analytical essay on Charles, coauthored by John Irvine, the student who had discovered the play.

A third part of the weekend was the announcement of a new $19.4 million Charles MacArthur Center for the American Theatre, to be built adjacent to Florida State University's Fine Arts Building. Funding would come, said the official announcement, from private sources. It didn't take a playwright's imagination to predict who the university was hoping one of those private sources would be.

Earlier, Fallon had sent Irvine down to Singer Island to tell John about his scholarly work on Charles and, in general, to help whip up MacArthur's enthusiasm for doing something at FSU to honor his brother. The young graduate student was not only impressed by the looks of the Colonnades, but awed by the cloud of money, power, and million-dollar deals that hung over MacArthur and his coffee-shop table, where the phone rang constantly.

Now John MacArthur, decades past financing *Theatre Arts* magazine and taking a flyer on Clare Boothe Luce's dramatic flop, found himself back in business as a theatrical backer of sorts. (Separate from the building fund, the center's $75,000 annual operating expenses would be covered mainly by John for the next few years.)

Of course, it was all about Charlie. Both Helen and John felt that Charles's fame rested too much on his reputation as bon vivant, practical joker, and gossip column regular and not enough on his stage and screenwriting talent. Sometimes his cowriters, including Ben Hecht, were given too much credit, they felt.

Charles MacArthur was much too modest in comparing his talent to those of other playwrights, for instance, Tennessee Williams, wrote Helen Hayes in her foreword to the book of selected plays. "It amused me later," she wrote, "when I was doing a play of Tennessee's, to have him tell me that Charles MacArthur had been an inspiration to him when he first began writing for the theatre. He also said, I remember, that Ben Hecht and Charlie had made it possible for him to write his kind of play 'because, you see, they took the corsets off the American theatre.'"

"Everybody loved my brother Charlie," wrote John in his graceful, 600-word biographical essay about his brother. "If he accepted an invitation, the party was an assured success." It has been years since he had been known as "Charlie's brother," John added poignantly. "This collection of his stage plays reminds me how I enjoyed sharing his theatrical world with him."

ONE OF THE more interesting by-products of the FSU project was the relationship that developed between MacArthur and Richard Fallon. After one of his trips to Tallahassee, MacArthur invited Fallon down to visit him at the Colonnades. "I can tell you a whole lot of things about Charlie," he promised. Fallon, of course, was eager to keep MacArthur interested in financial contributions to the developing new theatrical center. From MacArthur's point of view, Fallon, as a respected university dean, was a good-as-gold way to bring even more attention to Charlie. He encouraged the professor to tape their conversations, possibly hoping, Fallon speculated later, that he would someday write a book? a play?—something about Charlie. (Several years earlier MacArthur also had tentatively talked with Miami newspaperman Nixon Smiley about collecting and preserving material about Charlie.)

Fallon began to drive down to Singer Island several times a month, on occasion even making the trip in MacArthur's airplane. At first Sue Fallon sometimes accompanied her husband, but she soon became irritated at having to parry the passes of her host, who was still an unreconstructed womanizer.

But Richard Fallon was intrigued by this eccentric character, and undoubtedly flattered to be treated as a confidant—almost like a son— by the one of the country's richest men. John was still John, of course. *Do you want a drink? Something to eat?* MacArthur would ask. Fallon soon learned that after he finished his sandwich or his glass of MacArthur scotch that he would be presented with a bill. "Don't ever go to dinner with him," Helen had warned him. "You will end up paying."

Soon the stories Fallon was taping were as much about John as about Charlie. And John obviously enjoyed having an audience for his regular Colonnades coffee-shop minidramas. "Come here, Dick, I want you to see this," he would say about one thing or another going on at the hotel. One time, Fallon arrived at the hotel to find MacArthur deep in discussion with several of his lawyers. MacArthur insisted that "Dr. Fallon," as he liked to introduce him, join them at the table.

It seemed that the town of Palm Beach Shores was unhappy about a small addition being made to the hotel and demanded to see MacArthur's building permit. It so happened that this time MacArthur's paperwork was in order. Just show them your permit, advised the lawyers. Nope, said MacArthur, I want to go talk to the judge—"and you are coming along as my witness," he said, pointing at Fallon. (One of MacArthur's theories of jurisprudence was that you never showed up at court without your own, properly paid-for witnesses.)

Into a car they all piled. As they pulled up in front of the judge's office, the judge happened to be leaving. MacArthur approached him on the steps. Again, his lawyers told him to just show the judge his building permit, but MacArthur refused. "I want a jury trial," he insisted. But the judge, wise in the ways of the town's most prominent citizen, just laughed, shook his head, and said charges would be dismissed.

No jury trial? MacArthur was crushed. Curtain. The play had ended. The audience (Fallon) was wide-eyed. The lawyers would collect their usual fees for playing supporting roles. John, after all, had learned this sort of street theater from a master—his admired, cocky older brother, Charlie, who had once told an overbearing stage mother, "You don't understand, Madame. I was sent by God to be rude to you."

ON ST. PATRICK'S Day in 1973, Scranton, Pennsylvania, decided to honor Charles MacArthur, its most famous native son. John was invited to the festivities and even put on green pants and a top hat to ride in the parade. Earlier in the month, his own traditional birthday party had been held in Chicago. A guest at the party was John's older sister Marguerite, the second oldest of the MacArthur siblings, now age eighty-five. "Her memory is better than mine," said John later. Only John and his two sisters, Marguerite and Helen Bishop, were still living, and the beautiful Helen was incapacitated by Parkinson's disease. The rest of the MacArthur boys were all gone now. Telfer had died in 1960 at age sixty-eight, Alfred in 1967 at age eighty-two.

As for the more immediate family, from time to time John and his son Rod appeared to be trying to reestablish some sort of relationship. Rod and his French wife Christiane had three children: Gregoire, born in 1948, Solange, born in 1952, and Rick, born in 1956. Rod had moved his family to Florida to join his father's operations for a few years, living in what his father considered an extravagant house in West Palm Beach, but that hadn't worked out. When father and son were communicating—and sometimes they did that more easily in letters than in conversation—one or more of the grandkids would sometimes accompany Rod down to Florida, where they got to snorkel off Air Force Beach or visit the ranch.

But visits could be painful. There was the time, for instance, when Rod took Rick, then about thirteen, down to Florida as an emotional pawn, perhaps to tug at the *paterfamilias* heartstrings, while he (Rod) made a pitch for a percent of the businesses. Rod had worked for his father's bank after returning from Europe and then for Bankers Life, "reeled in" by vague promises of what would happen in the future. Rod felt that he had made a great deal of money for his father and his companies and because of that had now earned a share of the ownership, or at least a higher salary. But John would have none of it. "No, I don't think so," he said. "How about a car?" (Rod's son Rick later said that his father "chose to delude himself" about the kind of man John was, "but was more honest about him with me.")

The connection between John and his daughter Virginia was even more tenuous, even before a tragedy further shredded it. While living in Mexico City with her mother, Virginia had studied art and married Roberto de Cordova, an architect from El Salvador. Roberto and Virginia had four children—Robert, Gregorio, Juan, and Elizabeth.

Then in April 1973, twenty-one-year-old Greg disappeared while hitchhiking after his car broke down on his way to San Francisco to visit a girlfriend. Virginia appealed to her father for help with the search. John refused, saying it was just a case of a teenager trying to escape his parents' troubled marriage. The best face that could be put on this was that John *might* have been concerned about wide-scale family kidnappings. In fact, oilman J. Paul Getty's grandson would be kidnapped in Rome a few months later and a hefty ransom demanded. "I have fourteen other grandchildren, and if I pay one penny now, then I will have fourteen kidnapped grandchildren," Getty told the press. A hefty ransom was paid later, however, after the kidnappers mailed one of the Getty boy's ears to a Rome newspaper.

Nothing that gruesome developed (at least publicly) with the Cordova boy's disappearance, though he was never found and the family feared he had been robbed and murdered. (Rod would renew the search for his nephew five years later, at the time of John's death, hiring private investigators to hunt through police files and check jails. "If he's alive, which seems unlikely, he would be twenty-six years old.")

Yet John would sometimes go the extra mile for other people's children. When an assistant manager at the Colonnades received a telegram that her Marine son was missing in Vietnam, MacArthur told her not to worry, that he would probably turn up—and so he did, two days later. The young Marine told his mom that all kinds of people had been looking for him after receiving high-level calls from the Pentagon. MacArthur, she surmised, had called "somebody" in Washington.

There was a sad irony to anecdotes like this one, in light of examples of John as a disinterested father and grandfather. The fact was, he seemed to take pleasure in being around other people's kids, and they gravitated toward him.

One afternoon, Phil Lewis, a young real estate man in nearby Riviera Beach, got a call from "Mr. MacArthur," as he would always call him, inviting Lewis, his wife, and his entire family of nine children for dinner. It seemed that the Chicago office had been having trouble convincing a high-powered insurance salesman that he should come to work for Bankers Life. John decided to invite the man and his family down to the Colonnades for a week so they could talk. To John's surprise, it turned out that man had thirteen children, so the Lewis clan was invited to make it a real party.

Molly, who ran the Colonnades dining room, arranged all the kids by ages, and John and Catherine MacArthur waited on tables. The evening was a big success, and Bankers Life snagged the salesman. Later, Lewis discovered that his kids felt so at home at the Colonnades that they would drop by regularly to visit MacArthur. "I about fainted when I found out," said Lewis, who quickly put a stop to the impromptu visits.

Another time, Phil Lewis and his kids were invited to drive over to the ranch with MacArthur for the day. A van from the hotel came along with a smorgasbord lunch for the ranch hands and visitors. The only problem was the weather—unending rain. The Lewis youngsters, however, had a wonderful time playing football in the front yard of the ranch house, which quickly turned into a giant mud puddle. MacArthur was unperturbed and hosed the mud off his young visitors when it was time for them to clean up.

A few days later, Phil Lewis stopped by the hotel to apologize and thank MacArthur for being so tolerant of the kids, the mess, and the mud. "Never before or since did he raise his voice to me, but right then he did," Lewis would say later. "He let me have it with both barrels. He said, 'Those kids enjoyed themselves and so did I.'"

And then one of the world's wealthiest men, whose lifetime choices often had left his own family relationships in shambles, added, "You are truly a rich man."

CHAPTER 19

ROYAL SUMMONS

THE ENVELOPE ALONE immediately signaled that this was not an ordinary letter. The invitation inside read:

The President and Mrs. Ford
Request the pleasure of the company of
Mr. John D. MacArthur
For dinner on Wednesday evening, July 7, 1976
At 8 o'clock
On the occasion of the visit of Her Majesty Queen Elizabeth the Second
And
His Royal Highness Prince Philip Duke of Edinburgh

Even crusty old John MacArthur was impressed. "It's a beautiful engraved invitation. You'd cut your fingers if you slid 'em over it. I'm gonna have it framed," he told a reporter. A problem loomed, however. In one corner of the invitation were the words "White tie." MacArthur, who was generally allergic to *any* ties, was now going to have to deck himself out in white tie and tails like Fred Astaire—minus the top hat. MacArthur blustered at first that he was inclined to decline. Soon, however, the proprietor of a tuxedo shop in Palm Beach Gardens was at the Colonnades taking measurements for the clothes necessary for a formal state dinner.

Though many of the others on the invitation list of 200 were husbands and wives—Senator and Mrs. William Fulbright, Mr. and Mrs. Harold Geneen (ITT chairman), Mr. and Mrs. Henry J. Heinz II, Mr.

and Mrs. Reginald H. Jones (GE chairman), Dr. and Mrs. Melville B. Grosvenor (National Geographic Society)—it was not Mr. and Mrs. John D. MacArthur. Catherine's name might be on the foundation, but it was not on the invitation to the White House. Possibly this detail, as much as anything, indicated Catherine's increased avoidance of the public limelight—or the reality of the MacArthur marriage. Even a woman as reclusive as Catherine had become might well have been persuaded to dine at the White House with the queen.

Instead, John escorted his sister-in-law Helen Hayes, also on the guest list, along with such entertainment figures as Bob Hope, Greer Garson, Hermione Gingold, Cary Grant, Julie Harris, and Merle Oberon, several of whom, like Hope, were Brits by birth. John asked Helen to go ahead and make the necessary arrangements for hotel rooms and limo, after she insisted that it just wouldn't do for them to be delivered to the White House in a taxi.

The Ford-MacArthur friendship stretched back many years, including the time MacArthur, hamming it up, had acted as caddy while Gerald Ford played a round of golf on one of MacArthur's courses. There was another story that Jerry Ford, as a young lawyer in Michigan, had handled cases for Bankers Life on occasion. John, however, told reporters that he was sure that it was because of his World War I heroic exploits on behalf of Britain (as he often told the tale) that he was on the invitation list. (And, since it was an election year, it probably didn't hurt to have one of the country's wealthiest men drop by the White House.)

On Wednesday night, the Washington weather, drizzly during the afternoon, cleared as if by royal fiat as the queen, sparkling in diamonds, a vivid-yellow organza gown, and the royal blue sash of the Order of the Garter, arrived at the White House grounds. (A reporter noted that the only other guest in the diamonds competition was Happy Rockefeller, wife of Vice President Nelson Rockefeller.)

After the Fords and the royal couple greeted all 200 guests in a receiving line, dinner was served at large round tables decorated with bright summer flowers, in a large tent over the Rose Garden. The menu: New

England lobster en Bellevue with rémoulade sauce, saddle of veal, rice croquettes in baked golden baskets of woven-noodle dough, broccoli Mornay, and peach bombe with fresh berries. The balmy night, the twinkling Japanese lanterns in a beautiful garden setting; women in elegant gowns and their sartorially splendid escorts. It was not exactly John MacArthur's kind of party. But there were old friends for him to talk to, like Hope and Billy Graham.

While waiting in the receiving line, MacArthur had approached Graham. "Billy," John asked, "do you remember that university I wanted to build for you years ago? If we'd gone ahead with it, we would've had a great institution by this time. You made a mistake in not accepting it."

"I don't think so, John. I believe God led me," Graham, in a later speech, remembered telling MacArthur. "And he [MacArthur] said, 'I don't,' and turned and walked away."

After dinner the guests moved into the East Room to be entertained by comedian Hope and the pop musical group The Captain and Tennille. Good food and good entertainment had demolished the evening's precise timetable, and it was past midnight by the time of the evening's final ritual. President Ford—tall, still football-player trim, handsome in white tie and tails—and a radiant Queen Elizabeth II moved onto the dance floor as the Marine band played, to the amusement of many, "The Lady Is a Tramp."

That innocent musical gaff brought smiles. However, John's comments afterward to his hometown paper brought not the laughs he had, perhaps, been angling for, but rather outrage. He didn't have much to say about the diamond-tiara-wearing queen, other than that she was attractive from the neck up and outshone by First Lady Betty Ford. He had shaken hands with the royal couple, he reported, but "Helen did her squat" (curtsy).

Readers seemed irate about both the article's headline, "John D. Unimpressed by Her Majesty," and his comments, which they called "tacky," "tactless," and "ignorant," uttered by an "Ugly American" and "a man of colossal ego who feels himself to be far above the average mortal." Even though at the end of the article he was quoted as saying he was "honored and proud" to attend the affair, the reaction he drew was perhaps another example of MacArthur's tin ear. As often happened, he failed to grasp how his actions and statements would be received by others—in this case, not as you-can't-impress-me, antiroyalist homespun wit, but as rudeness.

The irony was that, in truth, he seemed to have been quite impressed by the royal event. "I was indifferent when I first heard I might be invited," he wrote to the White House a week after the dinner. "I am a country boy at heart and don't even like to wear a necktie, let alone a white one. However, the event will go down in my memory as the greatest affair I ever attended. I appreciated being met at the airport and all the other nice things you did. I will be eternally grateful to you."

Some time later, John and Helen Hayes both happened to be in Tallahassee at the same time. Helen stopped by to see her friend, Dick Fallon, and asked him to come with her to John's hotel. When they arrived, she began berating John for ignoring her repeated requests that he pay his share of the limo, hotel bill, and other Washington expenses. She wasn't leaving until he paid, she said. "Dick's here as my witness," she told him. Backed into the corner, John reluctantly wrote her a check. Down in Palm Beach Gardens, the man who had provided the full dress suit also had not been paid. Instead, the Colonnades manager arranged for him to get a week's vacation in the Bahamas.

THE QUEEN'S VISIT to this former colony during July 1976 was, of course, part of America's exuberant celebration of its two-hundredth birthday. The MacArthurs, John and Rod, had launched their own bicentennial fireworks a year earlier, involving, appropriately enough, the Revolutionary War hero, the Marquis de Lafayette.

After earlier failing to get the kind of raise in salary and other compensation from his father that he thought he had earned, Rod told himself that he alone would keep control of his next good idea. In addition to consulting for Citizens Bank and Bankers Life, Rod had been working for a small mail-order company of his father's called Macmart. He soon learned that convincing people to buy stereo systems with psychedelic lights and similar kitsch was harder than it looked.

However, one thing people seemed enthusiastic about buying by mail were commemorative plates, a hobby that extended back to 1895 and a Danish firm's production of a special blue-and-white Christmas plate with a scene called "Behind the Frozen Window." With the bicentennial a few years away, and with his good contacts in France, Rod decided to commission a set of plates honoring Lafayette, the young French general who came to the aid of the struggling Americans.

He went to his father with a proposal. If John would advance him start-up money, he would receive half the profits from the sale of the Lafayette plates (a limit that Rod said he carefully nailed down in writing). Buying an unused corporate shell from John for $700, Rod changed its name to Bradford Galleries Exchange, since one of his ideas also was to market his new company as an organized way for collectors to buy and sell their collectibles. By 1973, "Galleries" had been dropped from the name and The Bradford Exchange had issued its first "Current Quotations."

The d'Arceau-Limoges Lafayette Legacy Collection, a set of seven porcelain plates, depicted Lafayette in various scenes—including Lafayette signing up as a volunteer, the Battle of Brandywine, and the Battle of Yorktown. The collecting public, on a prebicentennial high, snapped up the plates, as Rod had predicted. This, in turn, caught John's attention, and he told his son (according to Rod's later recounting) that he wanted 51 percent ownership of the company. (No mere blood connection could change an almost Pavlovian lifetime habit of going for the throat of a possibly vulnerable business quarry.)

Rod said no, that was not our deal. Sometime later in 1974, he received a call from one of John's assistants, telling him that he was fired as a consultant for both the bank and Bankers Life. At that, Rod decided to replace the loss of this $30,000 in salary by bumping up his Bradford salary from $20,000 to $50,000.

That made John madder still. Rod offered to buy him out—$250,000, including past and future interest in the Lafayette plates. According to Rod, John had invested $115,000 in Bradford Exchange and now insisted on an outside audit and half of all the Lafayette plates income to date. That figure, the auditors reported, would be $175,000, which, of course, was less than the $250,000 Rod had originally offered.

Still there was no peace. One day in early spring 1975, Rod and his staff found themselves locked out of the suburban warehouse/offices they were using in one of John's buildings in a Chicago suburb. Rod had no access to Bradford's stock of plates, its computerized accounts and lists of customers, or money, since John had frozen the business's bank accounts. It was time for a counterattack—the "Great Crockery Raid," as Rod later enjoyed calling the skirmish. And in this bit of derring-do, he would show himself to be every inch his father's son.

On Monday, May 12, 1975, trucks pulled up to the warehouse in broad daylight, and Rod and his employees began loading plates. John's alarmed employees called the cops. Rod, who was prepared for this, showed the officers invoices and other paperwork that established him as owner of the inventory. The authorities were convinced and let the loading continue. Eventually, seven truckloads, including 25,000 plates, were moved to another building. In the end, father and son worked things out. After all, it was just a fight between accountants, grumbled John later.

Collectors continued to buy plates, and The Bradford Exchange announced 1975 revenues of $10 million and profits of $1.5 million. Three years later, the company would gross $35 million. Rod had made his own fortune.

WHEN HIGH-PROFILE, successful men reach a certain age, the public wants to know how they did it, could they do it again, could anybody else do it? The 1976 Guinness Book of World Records announced that the United States had four living billionaires: John Paul Getty, Howard Hughes, shipping tycoon and global investor Daniel K. Ludwig, and John D. MacArthur. Before the year was out, Hughes had died en route from Mexico to Houston; Getty had died in London. "D. K." Ludwig, considered by some to be nearly as mysterious as Hughes, was generally uncommunicative with the press. That left MacArthur at his table in the coffee shop, proud of being "the Accessible Billionaire," as a 1976 Canadian documentary called him, and mellower now as his seventies were waning.

But this mellowness still had limits—and he sure didn't want anybody using the P word. "Would you talk to us about the new John D. and Catherine T. MacArthur Foundation?" the documentary reporter asked. "No, you will be making me out as a philanthropist . . . I would be a sucker . . . it would be open season. . . ."

A Florida weekly newspaper sent a young reporter over to the Colonnades to find out if it was still possible to turn $10,000 into a million. MacArthur gave him some surprisingly thoughtful answers. "I'd use half the money to buy a business," he said. "If one of those good fast-food franchises is available, I'd buy it. That's a relatively safe way to get your foot in the door. Or I might use $5,000 to start my own franchise operation. But I'd never sink all my capital into one thing."

Using his own formula—"hard work, luck, and opportunism, in that order"—MacArthur would make this first business a success. "Then I would hire someone to run it, while I bought another business or two." That was the key, he continued, "compound business ventures," using profits from one to buy another and another. Once there was adequate income being produced by these small businesses, it would be time to look around for something bigger, say, a hotel "or any other business you can make profitable."

MacArthur took his customary swipe at the government. As this hypothetical big business took off and the million-dollar goal was getting close, "you probably should start showing some losses for the Internal Revenue Service. The government's going to get their piece of the action all along." The other problem, he added, would be finding competent, reliable employees. And yes, MacArthur said, he could do it all over again.

However, it would be "tougher" now, he had conceded to an earlier reporter who also had wanted his "formula" for business success. "There's too much government," he said, "and you need a rich uncle to get started." And at least as far as building an insurance empire was concerned, "you couldn't start from scratch as I did," he told yet another interviewer. "You'd need to have at least a million dollars before you could get a license to sell insurance in a state."

As he often did these days, MacArthur named luck as an important ingredient in his success. "You gotta be lucky and have the intelligence to know it's a break and then work like hell when things are breaking your way." MacArthur could now also afford to be open with reporters about his failures; for instance, his unsuccessful attempt to crash New York banking circles by becoming the largest stockholder (18 percent) of Security National Bank in Hempstead, Long Island. When the faltering bank was later sold (in early 1975) to Chemical Bank, MacArthur, who had invested about $32 million, came out with only about $7 million.

MacArthur's thoughts and comments seemed a bit fuzzier in November 1976, when he spoke at a big Palm Beach County business luncheon at the JDM Country Club (the new name of the former PGA layout). He delivered a "rambling speech," said the local paper the next day. This time he attributed his success to "seventy-nine years of good luck and the greatest mother in the world." He stayed healthy, he said, by eating "like my mother taught me. I clean the supper plate, eat whatever is on it."

Rambling speech? Thoughts of his early life and his mother? Events a week later showed that perhaps these were harbingers of serious medical problems. On November 23, 1976, MacArthur entered Good Samaritan Hospital in West Palm Beach, having "choked on an ice cube" and suffering from overwork, the press was told.

Two weeks later, in an exquisite bit of timing for someone as addicted to litigation as MacArthur, the district appeals court ruled against

MacArthur in the long-running Palm Beach soap opera pitting Mac-Arthur against his onetime tenant, Adeline Moffett, the impoverished widow of a Standard Oil board chairman. Because MacArthur was presently in the hospital "for a rest," he deserved extra time, said the court, to comply with its ruling that he supply an accounting of his net worth.

Shortly before Christmas, Catherine confirmed that MacArthur had suffered a "mild stroke." Aides publicly discounted any talk that his capacities had been affected. He was up, active, and making business decisions, they insisted. A reporter poking around at the Colonnades after MacArthur left the hospital found him walking toward an elevator, leaning heavily on the arm of a nurse. His answer to a question was reported to be "unintelligible."

In January, just two months after first entering the hospital, Mac-Arthur was feeling strong enough to put on a jacket and tie and go downstairs to pose for photographers with Rose Kennedy, his Palm Beach neighbor, who was delivering a speech at a learning resources conference at the Colonnades. Eventually, MacArthur would be able to get around a bit, but beyond a word or two, his speech would never return.

But a lifetime habit of running things dies hard. After his stroke, MacArthur would communicate by waving his arms, pointing, shaking, or nodding his head. Those around him usually understood what he wanted. When they didn't, not surprisingly the old man found it incredibly frustrating. There would be only a few more public appearances, and the first of those would be a gala celebration in Chicago for his eightieth birthday.

CHAPTER 20

AND WITH DIGNITY

THE ELDERLY MAN seated next to the window in coach on the flight from Florida to Chicago had finished his lunch. He looked at the meal tray of the stranger on the aisle. On it, there remained a piece of uneaten pecan pie. He poked his traveling companion, a young woman sitting between them. "Ask him if he is going to eat his pie," he told her. Once he was assured that the pie was not going to be consumed, John MacArthur leaned over and wrapped a paper napkin around the suddenly desirable bit of pastry. Checking to see if the stewardess was watching, he put it into his carry-on bag. "I'm Scotch," he said to the stranger with a grin, by way of explanation.

MacArthur's extreme frugality, a necessity in the save-every-penny early days, had morphed into theater and now possibly was slipping into weirdness. "He hated waste," explained the woman in the middle seat, Palm Beach newspaper reporter Gayle Pallesen, who was making the trip to cover MacArthur's gala eightieth birthday party in Chicago.

On the flight to Chicago, Pallesen and MacArthur were jammed into a three-across row in tourist class because that was how John always traveled. The back end of the plane will get there just as fast as the front end, he liked to say. It also saved money for Bankers Life. How could salesmen and other executives travel first class if the chairman was flying coach?

Another Florida reporter, Ray Mariotti, researching an investigative piece on MacArthur, experienced this frugality in action. Talking his way onto a commercial flight to a convention of several of MacArthur's companies, Mariotti was told by a MacArthur aide that this time John had a first-class ticket. Instead, John rode in tourist as he usually did. "I swapped with a guy waiting to get on the plane," MacArthur explained. "Some of my agents were on this plane and how would it look for me to be up-front while they were in the back."

That flight was actually a whistle-stop affair, Mariotti would write later, with stops in Tampa, New Orleans, and Houston. At each stopover, crowds of employees from the MacArthur "insurance family" who hadn't qualified for the trip to the sales convention could at least show up at the airport (with noisemakers and wearing party hats) and be photographed with the boss. "Those airport greetings seemed sincere and enthusiastic," wrote Mariotti. "Maybe it's just a trait of insurance men."

And that was the point of the annual Chicago MacArthur birthday parties as well, like the one to which MacArthur was heading in March 1977. They had become the keystone of the plaid-mad, fever-pitched sales month with its "March for MacArthur" and sales "turn-in" breakfasts, which MacArthur himself had started years earlier.

"Though we observe the calendar year in our day-to-day activities, in our hearts, the year begins when we step out proudly for JDM in March," sales vice president Russ Van Kampen had told the crowd several years earlier. And in those earlier, healthier years, MacArthur often would leave the Chicago celebrations and hopscotch around to other district events in other cities to shake hands and give out plaques and bonus checks to high-achieving salesmen, God bless 'em, who knew that this corporate reaffirmation and slap on the back was coming from one of their own.

But not this year. Just getting to Chicago was tough enough only four months after his stroke, and MacArthur had vacillated on whether to try to make the trip. Come he had, however, so there was added poignancy to this March 1977 event. Bankers employees filling the hotel ballroom realized that "The Skipper," one arm still useless, his words a bit hard to understand, might not be making it to these annual razzle-dazzle affairs too many more years. On the other hand, he was tough, the family was tough—why, sister Marguerite, eighty-nine years old now, had even made it to the event one more time, even with a broken arm and in a wheelchair.

Host Paul Harvey, who had been the radio voice of Bankers Life for more than thirty years, read telegrams from some of those who couldn't make the party (Bob Hope, Jack Nicklaus, Helen Hayes) and talked about what he had learned from MacArthur through the years ("You're never old till your dreams turn gray," and "We get up when we fall down"). "He's buttered the toast for the Harveys going on a third generation now," said Harvey, his voice wavering slightly. As usual, the festivities were awash in the green MacArthur tartan: plaid icing on the birthday cake, plaid jackets on the guest of honor and many of the guests, even a MacArthur nephew, Sandy (Alfred's son), in a family-plaid kilt. After his father died, Sandy MacArthur felt free to come to John's birthday parties where he could see his cousins and other relatives. Other nieces and nephews attended the birthday parties as well, including several of the next generation who had worked for Bankers at various times.

Catherine, whose health was also not so good these days, spent most of her time in their Colonnades apartment, kept company by the current MacArthur pets, toy poodles Happy and Mimi. She had been a voracious reader for years. One time she recommended a novel, *The Tontine*, a hefty, historical potboiler about a concept called a tontine—part lottery, part insurance—to visiting Miami newsman Nixon Smiley, who said he wanted to write about insurance. She also was fond of detective stories.

In earlier years Catherine had traveled some with her sister, Pat, who now had retired from handling Alfred's estate in Chicago, bought a condominium in the area, and spent much of the year in Florida. (John's idea of a joke one time had been to have some matchbooks printed up with the message that if you wanted a good massage, call this number—then he gave Pat's phone number. He considered his sister-in-law strait-laced and thought she ought to loosen up a little.)

Catherine generally seemed uncomfortable in the world beyond Bankers, or later, the Colonnades. She was interested in art, but she often would make a selection from the photographs that a gallery in Palm Beach would send to her. Other dealers would bring their wares to her at the hotel so that she could choose a Chinese vase, perhaps, or a small sculpture of jade or ivory for her collection of Oriental art and Lalique crystal.

One time, when Catherine and Paul Doolen's wife were shopping in Palm Beach, Mrs. Doolen took her into one of the elegant, expensive little dress shops for which the golden resort town was famous. Catherine was delighted, since she said she had never had the nerve to go into one of these shops. As the wife of one of the richest men in America, she could have bought and sold most of the other fashionable Palm Beach shoppers three times over, not to mention the intimidating saleswomen with turned-up noses. "She was as frugal as John, and perhaps some of his frugality rubbed off on her," said Mrs. Doolen later.

Palm Beach Post reporter Pallesen accompanied John MacArthur again later in 1977, when he was among the many Americans honored at the American Academy of Achievement banquet in Orlando. The number and the variety of guests on hand to inspire 300 of the country's high school honor students was impressive: legal stars Leon Jaworski, John Sirica, and Louis Nizer; author Alex Haley; actress Cloris Leachman; exercise guru Jack La Lanne; broadcaster Howard Cosell; as well as Hank Aaron, Stevie Wonder, and General Jimmy Doolittle. Television newscaster John Chancellor looked at the collection of achievers seated at the two long tables across the front of the room and cracked, "The inventor of the artificial kidney [Dr. Willem J. Kolff] is sitting next to the inventor of artificial chicken [Colonel Harland Sanders]." Helen Hayes was among the honorees as well, and when it came time for MacArthur to receive his plaque, she joined him onstage and made his speech for him.

The weekend's private cocktail party was off-limits to the press, but MacArthur didn't see any reason why Pallesen shouldn't attend. "Tell 'em you're my nurse," he said, a gambit that worked and was not far from the truth, since Catherine made sure the reporter took charge of John's medicine when they traveled together.

Artist LeRoy Neiman was on hand to do sketches of the honorees. "This man is at ease," he said as he made quick strokes on paper to capture the craggy face of the Florida billionaire. "Getty was always grouchy, like Rockefeller," said Neiman. MacArthur was "handsome" in a very classy way "like a Barrymore," he said, using felt-tipped pens to apply touches of his trademark bright colors to the sketch. "He has the theatric look. . . . You've got to give a man like that vigor."

That vigor, however, was fading. MacArthur could still sit in the sun at the Colonnades and feed the ever-growing flock of waddling ducks. Occasionally, when he could get someone to drive him, MacArthur would make the rounds of some of his local properties—the Palm Beach Gardens Holiday Inn, the JDM Country Club—where waiters and others would fuss over him. But one last visit to Buck Island Ranch was unsuccessful, with John, grouchy and uncommunicative, showing little interest in what had formerly delighted him.

The king might be nearing the end, but life in his financial kingdom continued.

Bankers Life and Casualty Company was now the nation's second-largest health and accident insurance underwriter, said its president, Robert Ewing. The company had a field force of close to 4,000 operating in forty-seven states (but not in California, New Jersey, or New York), plus the District of Columbia and the Canadian provinces of Ontario and Quebec. It had net earnings in 1976 of nearly $22 million and admitted assets of nearly $960 million. Later, at the end of 1977, the company's admitted assets would be pegged at $1.04 billion by insurance examiners. *Best's Insurance Reports* called the executive staff "capable and experienced."

In October 1977, the Biltmore Hotel in Palm Beach was sold for nearly $4 million more than MacArthur had paid for it. The buyer said he intended to hang a color photo in the lobby of the man who had kept the landmark from being torn down. John felt well enough to attend the signing and make a few jokes.

On the other side of the ledger, the Federal Trade Commission's investigation of a 1976 complaint against Bankers Life and others, for misrepresentations of waterless land for sale in central and southern Colorado, plodded along. (In May 1979, a consent order settling the complaint would be reached with the FTC. Bankers and codefendants, while agreeing to guarantee refunds and "cease and desist" from claiming, among other things, that lots were "a good and safe investment," would state that the signing of the agreement was "for settlement purposes only" and did not "constitute an admission . . . that the law has been violated." The refunds and debt cancellations of as much as $14 million were expected to be the largest cash settlement the commission had ever arranged. The agreement was also notable, said the commission, for holding a creditor of land sales, Bankers Life, responsible for making sure that all requested refunds were made.)

Also continuing was the Department of Housing and Urban Development (HUD) investigation of Holley by the Sea, a huge residential/resort community under development near Pensacola.

In early December, John MacArthur was admitted to Good Samaritan Hospital in West Palm Beach with suspected gall bladder trouble. MacArthur, never the easiest of hospital patients, insisted that he be allowed to return home for three days over the holidays. But after Christmas, weak as a kitten, he willingly returned to the hospital. Exploratory surgery in early January showed that the problem was inoperable cancer of the pancreas.

MacArthur was told the truth—"I never fooled him," said his physician and friend, Dr. Donald Warren, at the press conference at the Colonnades that Catherine requested be held "so there would be no misinformation" about her husband's illness. "I expect he will expire within two weeks," said Dr. Warren. Paul Doolen explained that the doctor was following written directives MacArthur had given him several years earlier that he be allowed "to die painlessly and with dignity" if he should be diagnosed with a terminal illness. (In 1972, after visiting his sister, Helen Bishop, John had written a letter to Doolen about "the cruelty that we, as enlightened citizens, force upon our fellow men. . . . When I last saw David Sarnoff I regretted that anyone would force him to continue to breathe when all of his physicians conceded he would never recover his health.")

Newspapers, particularly those in Chicago and Florida, began a MacArthur deathwatch. Articles reviewed the good, the bad, and the astonishing aspects of the old billionaire's life. The family gathered around. At John's bedside were Catherine and Rod, who said that several months earlier he and his father had patched up their "strained" relationship. Pat Hyland arrived to be with her sister Catherine. Virginia flew in from Mexico on Wednesday evening, but by the time she got to the hospital Thursday morning, her father was no longer able to recognize her.

John MacArthur died shortly after midnight, Friday, January 6, 1978, at 2:12 A.M. The sun came up, and at the Colonnades Beach Hotel the flag was lowered to half-staff. In Chicago, an announcement over loud speakers told employees at Bankers Life that MacArthur had died. And just so there would be no misunderstanding among employees that there might be a day off in his memory, the voice on the loud speaker continued, "In accordance with Mr. MacArthur's wishes, it will be business as usual."

CHAPTER 21
GENIUS

IT HAD TO bring a chuckle to the departed spirit of John D. Mac-Arthur that even in death he could get a good fight going. It was March 6, 1979, and a group had gathered at a Chicago Ramada Inn near O'Hare Airport to toast the memory of the departed friend/relative/boss on what would have been his eighty-second birthday. The complication was that another group also had planned a wake in his honor, this one a moveable feast in June, scheduled to start in Chicago and move on to Florida.

John had made it clear that he did not want a typical funeral. He had planned on donating his body to a medical school so that medical education "should be furthered by the use of my remains." But the ravages of disease had made that bequest impractical, so instead his body was cremated and the ashes scattered from an airplane flying over the Gulf Stream off Florida's Atlantic coast.

In his will (eighteen pages, four codicils) filed in Chicago the day of his death, MacArthur had said that he didn't want a funeral. "I am mindful of the fact that most people attend funerals only as a matter of duty and in order to be seen by others in attendance," he had said in the document, dated 1963. "But it would not be contrary to my wishes if my wife schedules a memorial service or function to be held at a convenient place a month or two following my death, so that my friends and relatives who really wish to attend such a gathering can plan on it in an orderly manner." Perhaps with "a drink or two," he continued, they could "reminisce as people like to do, over past events and departed friends."

What John had in mind was an old-fashioned "Irish wake kind of thing," said son Rod, and the rather sedate March Ramada Inn affair hosted by Catherine and the Bankers Life company—"a little pep talk on how to sell more insurance"—did not fit the bill, he claimed. Instead, Rod announced that he, his sister Virginia, and his aunt, Marguerite, would be hosting a party in June that would begin in Chicago (so ninety-two-year-old Marguerite could partake), then move, via chartered plane, down to Palm Beach Gardens.

Catherine said she opposed such a party, that she would not attend, and that the estate probably would not pay for it. Bill Kirby told a Chicago reporter he had "no comment" about whether the estate would pay for a second party. If the estate won't, "then I will have to," said Rod.

The June wake was scaled back a bit when the number of acceptances was lower than expected, and just a section of an airplane, rather than a whole chartered plane, was reserved for the flight to Florida after a luncheon in Chicago. "This is what my father would have wanted," said Rod as he looked around at the 200 guests, ice sculpture, red roses, and fancy food in the Palm Beach Gardens Holiday Inn. (Rod had bought the hotel from the MacArthur estate.) "It's a hell of a lot more interesting than a funeral," said John's nephew Sandy, Alfred's son. "I think John had the right idea."

However, disagreements more serious than the size of a party had already begun to surface during the year following MacArthur's death. Some of it was a push-pull between Rod, primarily, and other directors of the new John D. and Catherine T. MacArthur Foundation, with foundation assets eventually determined to be $2 billion by 1983. (By the end of 2004, the MacArthur Foundation would have assets of $5.023 billion and be ranked eleventh in the United States in the 2006 *Foundation Directory*. This was after the arrival on the philanthropic scene of the giant Bill and Melinda Gates Foundation, with assets of $28.8 billion.)

In December 1978, eleven months after John's death, the John D. and Catherine T. MacArthur Foundation had made its first two grants, awarding $50,000 to Amnesty International and the same amount to the

California League of Cities. Louis Feil had resigned his seat on the foundation's board of directors because of a conflict of interest involving his partnership with MacArthur in some of Bankers real estate subsidiaries. There were suggestions that other of the Bankers people on the board (Bill Kirby, Paul Doolen, and Bankers president Robert Ewing) should do the same because of conflicts of interest. Nonsense, they said—John wanted people he knew and trusted directing this foundation. Verbal scuffles (and even lawsuits) about new board members, the nature of grants, and the sale of MacArthur properties would continue long into the future.

The keystone of the MacArthur fortune, the Bankers Life and Casualty stock, had gone to the foundation as planned. But there was much else to be distributed. By terms of the will, stock in Citizens Bank and Trust Company (valued at more than $415 million) would go to another foundation, The Retirement Research Foundation. The rest of the probated estate (estimated at about $60 million in 1987) would be split, with half going to second wife Catherine—actually to a trust she had established—and half to be divided into trusts for John's two children, Rod and Virginia. There were several small bequests, including $5,000 to his first wife, Louise, and to a niece, Janet, Helen Bishop's daughter.

In Tallahassee, there was stunned disbelief that John had left no funding for the Charles MacArthur Center for the American Theatre at Florida State University, or at least a memorandum of intent to the foundation. Later appeals to the foundation would meet with no success. Nearly eight months after John's death the theater center's last salaried employee was dropped from the payroll. Its collections of American theater memorabilia and documents eventually would be boxed up, roam from location to location like some ghostly Flying Dutchman, and in time be partially dispersed.

Within days of MacArthur's death, the states of Florida and Illinois, rubbing their hands together in anticipation of estate taxes projected to be as much as $100 million, began wrangling over John's legal place of residency. MacArthur had carefully maintained his Illinois residency and that was where he voted, said his attorneys. Doesn't matter, said

Florida's attorney general (who was running for governor). He cited a 1977 Florida law that said anyone living twelve consecutive months in Florida during the two years preceding death was a Florida resident, no matter where he voted. In addition to Illinois and Florida, the state of Texas, where MacArthur also had property, would eventually receive some tax revenue from the estate. (The tax-hating tycoon would have loved a Florida newspaper headline: "Tax from Billionaire's Estate Low.")

Slowly, much of the MacArthur Florida property was moving into other hands, or at least into new management. Buck Island Ranch, John's favorite getaway place west and north of Lake Okeechobee, was leased by the foundation for one dollar a year to the Archbold Biological Station, a nearby central Florida nonprofit research facility to become the MacArthur Agro-ecology Research Center. Here researchers, using the bedrooms of the ranch house as offices and spreading their site maps out in the large central room, would study how to make a working cattle ranch compatible with new ecological concerns about water quality and wildlife habitat. ("Mr. Mac would hate those weeds in the canal," said former ranch manager Dan Childs many years later, driving a visitor around the ranch. The weed killers MacArthur had insisted on using, of course, wouldn't pass today's environmental muster.)

Air Force Beach, where John MacArthur and countless others went skinny-dipping, became MacArthur Beach State Park. Grandson Rick MacArthur would fume later about a memorial plaque near the park's nature center that honored John and ignored his father, Rod, who, he felt, deserved the credit for saving the valuable stretch of oceanfront land for the public to enjoy. William Kirby, however, said that one of the few specific suggestions John made about what became of his land was that this beach remain public. "That foundation you are talking about could give it to the folks," said John, according to Kirby.

In 1980 the foundation donated eighty-two acres of beachfront to the public, and the state and county jointly bought Air Force Beach from the foundation for $23 million. Rod MacArthur served as chairman of the joint state/foundation design committee for several years, and the park at the north end of Singer Island, with coral reef where the Mac-Arthur grandchildren once snorkeled, opened to "the folks" in 1989.

John's money, wreathed in political conservatism, had come in handy in 1980 when Rod and Rick teamed up to save the 130-year-old, "fashionably left-wing" *Harper's Magazine*. The MacArthur and Atlantic Richfield foundations were persuaded to fund a nonprofit foundation to take over the magazine, and Rick, a young Chicago journalist, was named publisher.

THERE WOULD BE many such fascinating ironies in the future as the MacArthur Foundation, moving beyond titanic early board battles, eventually settled down to fund a broad and impressive sweep of global programs and organizations, some of which could be characterized as social-activist and (take a deep breath) liberal. The man who made the money might shake his head or let loose a string of salty comments. But who's to know? It is tempting but often a mistake to say with confidence how someone who has died would react to this or that later development.

Gayle Pallesen, the reporter who spent much time with MacArthur in his last year and a half, thought the real paradox was that a man as hands-on in running his affairs as MacArthur would decide to let others make the decisions about his money. MacArthur told another reporter, "I've seen too many people, including Henry Ford, try to administer their estates from the grave. You have changing times. Besides, you lay down rules and people don't follow them. So I'll trust to the Almighty that my trustees will do more good for the country than I would."

No program of the John D. and Catherine T. MacArthur Foundation would make its name better known—particularly among those in the academic, science, and arts communities—than the MacArthur Fellows Program. "They [the foundation] hit some kind of sympathetic chord when they did the 'genius awards,'" commented Robert Bothwell, executive director of the National Committee for Responsive Philanthropy, just four years after the program began in 1981. Every year, an impressively large sum of money (in 2006, a half-million dollars over a five-year period) would be given—no strings attached—to two dozen or so medical researchers, teachers, glass bead artists, poets, Mayan epigraphists, or any individual with sufficient creative potential, as determined by a secret committee of "selectors."

Because of this program, the MacArthur name would enter the national vocabulary as shorthand for achievement. People win "a MacArthur" just as they win a Guggenheim, a Pulitzer, or a Fulbright. Yet, despite this program's high profile, only a small percentage of the foundation's annual grants go to these genius awards. (The foundation is not fond of this term. Selectors look for qualities besides genius, such as "persistence in the face of personal and conceptual obstacles," explains the foundation's website in answer to a question of why the fellows grants are not just called by the name by which they are generally known.)

John D. MacArthur, of course, is the man behind the genius awards only in the sense that he is the man behind the *money* behind the genius awards. In an amazing "after you, Alfonse," bit of cooperation, Rod MacArthur and William Kirby would generally share credit with one another for making the idea a reality. In August 1978, Kirby brought to the board an editorial in a medical journal by an innovative cardiologist, Dr. George Burch, which suggested that thinkers needed time and space to think. "Investigators should receive minimal support and be left alone without the annoyances and distractions imposed by grant applications, reviewing committees, and pressure to publish," wrote Burch.

Rod was quickly on board with the idea, explaining to *Newsweek*, "Albert Einstein could not have written a grant application saying he was going to discover the theory of relativity. He needed to be free."

ROD HIMSELF DIDN'T live to see the burgeoning public fascination with the MacArthur Fellows Program. He died in late 1984, a week shy of his sixty-fourth birthday, from cancer of the pancreas, the same disease that had killed his father, John. Rod's sister, Virginia MacArthur de Cordova, John's only other child, died in 2002. Divorced from her husband, she had lived for many years relatively modestly in Mexico, giving English lessons and taking care of her mother, Louise. Greg Cordova, the son who disappeared, was never located, as far as is known. Louise Ingalls MacArthur, John's first wife, died in 1979, a year after John's death.

Catherine T. MacArthur died in Palm Beach Shores in 1981, also of cancer. She was seventy-three. Her bequests exceeded $25 million to various Palm Beach County organizations, including Palm Beach Atlantic College, St. Mary's Hospital, Good Samaritan Hospital, and the Animal Rescue League of the Palm Beaches.

John's elder sister, Marguerite MacArthur Wiley, the last surviving MacArthur sibling, died in 1986 at the age of ninety-nine. Helen Hayes, Charlie's widow and John's sister-in-law, died in 1993. The Colonnades Beach Hotel, remodeled a couple of times, was eventually torn down in the early 1990s, and a luxury hotel/condominium built on the site. The ocean and sunrises remained unchanged.

Bankers Life and Casualty was sold by the MacArthur Foundation in 1984 to ICH Corporation, and in 1992 it passed into the hands of Conseco, an insurance-industry holding company almost the match for Bankers in terms of controversy and colorful officers. In 1993 the Bankers home office was moved into fancy digs in Chicago's massive Merchandise Mart. The maze of old headquarters buildings on Chicago's northwest side was demolished and a nice, if plain, six-story brick senior living facility built on the site at Lawrence and Kenneth avenues.

The massive brass doors of the original bank building at 4444 West Lawrence Avenue, through which decades of Bankers employees and customers had walked, were carefully salvaged and installed in the new

Bankers lobby, along with a commemorative plaque. Possibly an old-timer or two remembered John MacArthur's philosophy, expressed in a 1974 memo to Paul Doolen: "I am wide open for any suggestion that will improve our operation," he wrote, "but still believe brick and mortar will not sell insurance. Manpower plus leads will do the job, unless we waste our money on nonsense."

LOCATION OF COLLECTIONS CITED

Bankers Life and Casualty. Company archives are at the insurance company's home office in the Merchandise Mart, Chicago, Illinois.

Fallon Tapes. The School of Theatre, Florida State University, Tallahassee, Florida, has transcripts and original tapes of interviews with John D. MacArthur conducted by the school's one-time dean, Richard Fallon. Page numbers refer to transcript pages. Page 40 is the last page with original numbers. Page numbers in parentheses are working numbers added by author.

Graymont Papers. Bailey Library at Nyack College, Nyack, New York, has extensive interview transcripts and other research material collected by Barbara Graymont and John Taylor in the preparation of their book, *The MacArthur Heritage: The Story of an American Family,* privately published by the John D. and Catherine T. MacArthur Foundation in 1993. Page numbers of Taylor interviews refer to transcript pages.
Transcripts of the John Taylor interviews are also in the archives of the MacArthur Foundation, 140 S. Dearborn, Chicago, Illinois.

Illinois Division of Insurance. Archives for the division (sometimes, through the years, called the Illinois Department of Insurance) are at the Illinois Department of Financial and Professional Regulation in Springfield, Illinois.

Palm Beach County (Florida) Collections. The Historical Society of Palm Beach County, Paramount Building, Palm Beach, maintains extensive material (much of it clippings) concerning John MacArthur and the Colonnades. Other material (also much of it clippings) is available at the local village history room of the North Palm Beach Public Library, in North Palm Beach, and at the Palm Beach County Library, North County Regional Branch, in Palm Beach Gardens.

Smiley Papers. The Research Center of the Historical Museum of Southern Florida, Miami, Florida, houses files containing the notes and writings of Miami reporter and author Nixon Smiley, who did extensive interviews with John D. MacArthur.

NOTES

Numbers on the left refer to pages

CHAPTER 1—RANSOMING THE RUBY

4 *said it would be:* Details of the story of the ruby's recovery and theft are from the New York *Daily News*, July 3, 1965, and ongoing coverage (the man in the phone booth was a *Daily News* reporter); other sources are *New York Times*, July 3, 1965, and ongoing coverage; *New York Herald Tribune*, September 3, 1965, and ongoing coverage; JDM to editor, *New York Herald Tribune*, September 9, 1965; Smiley Papers; Allan Kuhn, Jack Murphy, Roger Clark, as told to Fred Ferretti, "How We Stole the Star of India," *True*, December 1965; Jack Roth, "The Beachboy Caper," *Esquire*, September 1965; Francis P. Antel, *Ransom and Gems: The DeLong Ruby Story;* author visit to Morgan Hall of Minerals and Gems, American Museum of Natural History, New York, NY.

5 *billionaires:* Frederick Allen, *Atlanta Journal Constitution*, January 7, 1978; individual names arranged by death dates, not by size of fortune.

6 *enter the ranks . . . at number four:* "50 Largest Foundations by Assets," *The Foundation Directory*, 8th ed. (1981), xi (citing 1979 fiscal information). The John D. and Catherine T. MacArthur Foundation listed assets of $862 million to be ranked fourth on the list. Earlier, MacArthur Foundation had been listed as fifth largest in Charles W. Bell's special report on foundations in the *New York Daily News*, April 15, 1979, based on "tentative assets of $750 million, pending final official appraisal." At that point the W. K. Kellogg Foundation was in the top four.

Nigeria . . . digital age: "Report on Activities 1999," The John D. and Catherine T. MacArthur Foundation, 88; http://www.digitallearning.macfound.org/site/.

7 *assistant director:* Joseph Chamberlin, interview with author.

8 *tax deduction:* Louis S. Auchincloss to JDM, October 19, 1965; Joseph M. Chamberlain to JDM, October 20, 1965; JDM to Joseph M. Chamberlain, December 10, 1965; file 1161, Central Archives, Library, American Museum of Natural History, New York, NY.

process server: Nixon Smiley, "A Man Involved in Money," *Miami Herald Sunday Magazine,* November 7, 1965.

9 *"contribution to society":* JDM to Chamberlain, December 10, 1965.

   advertising/PR bargain: William Hoffman, *The Stockholder,* 150.

10 *their tenacity:* Barbara Graymont and John Taylor, *The MacArthur Heritage,* 79.

CHAPTER 2—BREAKING THE SOD

12 *Red Fife, Golden Drop:* F. L. Dickinson, "Prairie Wheat: Three Centuries of Wheat Varieties in Western Canada," (Winnipeg: Canada Grains Council, n.d.)12.

   Georgiana: This is the spelling generally used for the name—in a letter written by her future husband, in her death certificate (filled out by one of her sons), and in the name used by another of her sons for *his* daughter. Yet curiously, on the front of her own diary her name is spelled "Georgina," possibly in William's handwriting (Diary, file-Georgiana's Diary, box #1, Graymont Papers).

   southeastern corner: Christie Wood, Saskatchewan Archives Board, Saskatoon, SK, to author.

   lived in a tent . . . small cabin: William Telfer McArthur [sic], "Application for Homestead Patent," county of Turtle Mountain, province of Manitoba, July 17, 1885.

   "break" . . . ten acres: Johnnie Bachusky, "Saskatchewan Ghost Towns, Hatton," available at http://www.ghosttownpix.com/sask/towns/hatton.shtml.

13 *Manitoba . . . new ranch:* "Western Land Grants (1870–1930)," Charles Welstead (Liber 93, Folio 212). National Archives of Canada, ArchiviaNet, available through http://www.collectionsCanada.ca/02/0201_e.html.

   "the Almighty": William T. McArthur [sic], "A Spiritual Autobiography," *The Alliance Weekly,* June 13,1931, 376.

   "I am converted": Ibid., 377.

14 *lack of spiritual growth:* Ibid.

   soon marry . . . Jane: Jane Welstead, Dominion Statutory Declaration, October 9, 1890, Saskatchewan Archives, Saskatoon, SK. Jane, wife of Charles Welstead, identifies William Telfer MacArthur as her younger brother in this document. The purpose of the declaration was to determine whether William, though born in New York State, had moved to Canada with his British parents at the age of ten months and was, therefore, a British subject. William was confirming his citizenship status to document his patent (title) to his Saskatchewan homestead, probably for the sale of land or granting of right-of-way to Canadian Pacific Railway. William was living in Rochester, New York, at the time.

gluttonous goals: Georgiana MacArthur Hansen, interview with John Taylor, October 8, 1987, RG013/SE001/SS001, archives, MacArthur Foundation; Professor Marshall Gregory to author. Dickens's admirable title character, of course, was not of that ilk.

frontier worship services: McArthur, "A Spiritual Autobiography," 377.

15 *"shall be satisfied":* William T. MacArthur to Alfred Welstead, October 21, 1883, box #2, Graymont Papers.

helped with the delivery: Hansen interview with Taylor, October 8, 1987, 2.

Wild West Show: Graymont/Taylor, *The MacArthur Heritage*, 88, note 11.

have many ponies: Edward MacArthur to John Taylor, October 8, 1987, 2, RG013/SE001/SS001, archives, MacArthur Foundation.

"did not favor us": McArthur, "A Spiritual Autobiography," 377

16 *told Georgiana:* Ibid.

"want no more": Georgiana MacArthur's Diary, (13).

probably in 1894: Graymont/Taylor, *The MacArthur Heritage*, 89, note 6.

CHAPTER 3—BABY JOHN

18 *midwife:* Leora Huttar, interview with John Taylor, file-Interviews by John Taylor, box #1; list of photographs, box #2, Graymont Papers.

19 *during the year: Wilkes-Barre Record Almanac*, 1897, 57.

religious home: William McArthur [sic], "A Spiritual Autobiography," *The Alliance Weekly*, June 13, 1931, 378.

one of his sisters: Ibid.

"different work": "Christian Missionary Alliance Canadian Founder Dr. A.B. Simpson," http://www.rrac.ca/alliance/founder.html, accessed February 11, 2002.

20 *"rare bird": Alliance Weekly*, October 23, 1957, 7; Graymont/Taylor, *The MacArthur Heritage*, 20.

21 *covered . . . with her dress:* Lois Wiley Zimmerman (daughter of Marguerite MacArthur), interview with John Taylor, 2, file-MacArthur Grandchildren, box #1, Graymont Papers.

"pathetic indeed": "A Boy, a Musket, and Death," *Wilkes-Barre (PA) Record*, October 11, 1897; *Wilkes-Barre Record Almanac*, 1897, 56. In both papers, the children's names and ages are wrong.

"God of rest": Georgiana MacArthur Diary, probably 1889, (17), file-Georgiana's Diary, box #1, Graymont Papers.

"care of them": Ibid., (28)

22 *"gave me plenty"*: Ibid., (32–33).

23 *young . . . Billy Graham:* Excerpt from After-Dinner Remarks, Dr. Billy Graham, prior to dedication of the Graham Center, Wheaton, IL, September 15, 1980, file-Taylor John, box #1, Graymont Papers. Twenty-one-year-old Graham was in the audience when William MacArthur addressed the 1944 Annual Council of Christian and Missionary Alliance. John Taylor was also at that conference (John Taylor to Barbara Graymont, February 19, 1988, file-Taylor John). William MacArthur also had spoken at the Florida Bible Institute in Tampa while Graham was a student there (T. W. Wilson to John Taylor, file-Graham Billy, box #1, Graymont Papers).

"as my mother": Fallon Tapes, 9.

CHAPTER 4—LIFE WITH FATHER

24 *episode :* Ben Hecht, *Charlie,* 26; Helen Hayes with Sandford Dody, *On Reflection,* 155.

"available and accepting": Judith S. Krom to Jay Mapstone, January 31, 1989, box #2, Graymont Papers.

25 *"throwing pitch"*: Anita Bailey, interview with John Taylor, file-Interviews by John Taylor, box #1, Graymont Papers.

"muscular Christianity": Joan Malick. "The Sex-Role Self-Perception of Mega-Church Pastors and the Attributes of Leadership." Ph.D. diss., Union Institute and University, Cincinnati, OH, 1996; Margaret Lamberts Bendroth, *Fundamentalism and Gender* (Yale University Press, 1996).

eye on them: Dorothy Turner Ellenberger, interview with John Taylor, 2, RG013, SE001, SS001, archives, MacArthur Foundation.

26 *"the Lord"*: Hecht, *Charlie,* 26; Hayes, *On Reflection,* 156; Graymont/Taylor, *The MacArthur Heritage,* 30; John Taylor, in interview with author, said that John MacArthur, whom he interviewed several times, never indicated to him that Charlie's remembrances about William were wrong.

boys: Hayes, *On Reflection,* 156.

"to Him": "The Acts," Parlor Evangelist, September 1936, as quoted by Graymont/Taylor, *MacArthur Heritage,* 42.

"childhood wish": Freud as quoted by Daniel Boorstin, *The Discoverers,* 622.

career in business: Graymont/Taylor, *MacArthur Heritage,* 28.

27 *"new big rich"*: Stewart Alsop, "America's New Big Rich," *Saturday Evening Post,* July 17, 1965. Billionaire Daniel K. Ludwig, wouldn't agree to be interviewed, writes Alsop.

1905 . . . insurance company: Alfred MacArthur obituary, *Chicago Tribune*, December 14, 1967.

"fastest con in the West": Hank Johnston, *Death Valley Scotty: The Man and The Myth.*

tourist attraction: Ibid., 32–33; Edward MacArthur, interview with John Taylor, RG013/SE001/SS001, archives, MacArthur Foundation; http://www .inn-california.com; http://www.deathvalleychamber.org.

28 **Alfred had married:** Though Alfred gave 1909 as the year of his first marriage, his daughter, Georgiana, thought the date inside the ring she inherited from her mother, Josephine, read 1906 (interview with John Taylor, RG013,SE001,SS001, archives, MacArthur Foundation).

high school classes: Jean Guarino, *Yesterday: A Historical View of Oak Park, Illinois*, vol. 1, 86–87.

architectural concepts: Oak Park Area Visitor Guide, 7; Frank Lloyd Wright Commissions, http://www.prairiestyles.com/wright.htm.

their children: Georgiana MacArthur Hansen, interview with Don Kalec, June 1, 1977, collection no. Arch2006.09, Research Center, Frank Lloyd Wright Preservation Trust, Oak Park, IL.

lifelong friends: Alfred MacArthur correspondence with Frank Lloyd Wright, 1926–1940, collection no. Arch2006.09, Frank Lloyd Wright Preservation Trust.

business manager: Guarino, *Yesterday: A Historical View of Oak Park*, 138.

29 **"loved by everybody":** Edna Davidson, interview with John Taylor, file-Interviews by John Taylor, box #1, Graymont Papers.

"oddball": Ibid.

to hear them tell it . . . full of mischief: Robert Ekvall, interview with John Taylor; Frank Marten, interview with Brad Hess, file-Other Interviews, box #1, Graymont Papers.

"needed their father": George Paul Simmonds to John F. Taylor, June 24, 1987; the comment "that man hit me" is Simmonds to Taylor, quoting Wilson Memorial Academy student Mary Harver, Graymont Papers.

30 **father's clothes:** Simmonds to Taylor, again quoting Harver.

dormitory: Graymont/Taylor, *MacArthur Heritage*, 35.

dancing: Ibid., 34, 36; Hecht, *Charlie*, 27.

illness: Graymont/Taylor, *MacArthur Heritage*, 37; Wilson Memorial Academy grade records.

deportment: Wilson Memorial Academy grade records, John MacArthur, 1911–12 and 1912–13, file-John Roderick MacArthur (possibly misfiled), box # l, Graymont Papers.

a lie: Marten, interview with Hess.

eighth grade: grade records, John MacArthur; Graymont/Taylor, *MacArthur Heritage,* 37.

CHAPTER 5—THE COMPETITOR

34 *boglike pool:* Fred LeBrun, "The Hudson River Chronicles, Part I," *Times Union,* September 15, 1998, available at www.timesunion.com/specialreports/hudsonriver/1/.

choppy water: *Nyack Evening Star,* July 17, 1914.

35 *Wilson W was his:* *Nyack Evening Star,* July 21, 1914; *The Nyacks and Piermont, 1909–1910* (Newburg, NY: Breed Publishing Co.), 132, Local History Room, Nyack Public Library. The site of the Tappan Zee Inn (which burned in 1932) is just north of the west end of the Tappan Zee Bridge, opened in 1955.

Bible classes: John MacArthur grade reports, Wilson Memorial Academy, 1911–1912 and 1912–1913, file-John Roderick MacArthur, box #1, Graymont Papers.

"deteriorating health": Graymont/Taylor, *The MacArthur Heritage,* 38.

first year in high school: Later articles about JDM usually called him either an eighth-grade dropout or someone whose education didn't go beyond the eighth grade. Grade reports at Nyack College show he completed one year of high school.

36 *"see them":* Ben Hecht, *Charlie,* 30.

intestinal cancer: Death certificate, Department of Health, City of New York, February 16, 1915. The year of Georgiana's birth (1857) is recorded but not the month and day, file-Vital Records, box #2, Graymont Papers.

mail . . . from Nyack: Fallon Tapes, (59).

deception: Ibid.

"sorrowing friends": *Alliance Weekly,* February 27, 1915, 349, box #2, Graymont Papers.

"all round the world": *Annual Council Report of the Christian and Missionary Alliance,* as quoted by Graymont/Taylor, *MacArthur Heritage,* 39.

St. Catharines, Ontario: Graymont/Taylor, *MacArthur Heritage,* 39.

Peace Chapel: *Alliance Weekly,* February 27, 1915, 349.

37 *making bayonets:* Duncan Groner, "Meet John D. MacArthur, America's Least Known Billionaire," United Press International (UPI), March 19, 1972.

"working in Chicago—1915": Hecht, *Charlie,* 32.

steadying influence: Graymont/Taylor, *MacArthur Heritage,* 44.

"Send him to me": Fallon Tapes, (60).

into the field: Fallon Tapes, 9.

in a race: Fallon Tapes, (61). In the retelling, JDM does not say who won.

38 *buy the . . . paper:* Jean Guarino, *Yesterday: A Historical View of Oak Park, Illinois,* 138. Telfer's Pioneer Press eventually published nearly a dozen suburban papers in North and Westside Chicago.

boring: Groner, UPI, March 19, 1972.

worked more hours: Fallon Tapes, 10.

moving in with Charlie: Graymont/Taylor, *MacArthur Heritage,* 45. Another reason for the move, John would sometimes say, was that Alfred and Telfer thought John could better keep Charlie under control if he spent more time with him.

Charlie's big story: Fallon Tapes, 40; Guarino, *Yesterday,* 152.

$20 a week: Fallon Tapes, 31.

not a newspaperman: Fallon Tapes, 29.

39 *ordered everbody home:* Illinois State Military Museum, Historical Events, Mexican Border War, http://www.il.ngb.army.mil/Museum/HistoricalEvents/ MexicanB.htm.

"victorious banners" . . . amused: Hecht, *Charlie,* 15–16.

40 *enlisted . . . in U.S. Navy:* Department of the Navy, Service Record, John Donald MacArthur, enlistment date May 21, 1917, Chicago, IL; place of birth, Pittston, PA; SN 146 34 06, Military Personnel Records, St. Louis, MO.

legal age of enlistment: Kevin Flanagan, librarian, American Legion National Headquarters, interview with author.

"dementia praecox": Report of Medical Survey, October 9, 1917, Medical Survey Discharge, dated October 23, 1917, Service Record, Military Personnel Records. "He is not a menace to himself or to the community," added the Board of Medical Survey. The former seaman was not recommended for reenlistment or for a Good Conduct Medal.

milkman: Jean MacArthur Looby, interview with John Taylor, 4, file-Interviews MacArthur Grandchildren, box #1, Graymont Papers.

41 *Royal Flying Corps:* AIR 76/312 RAF officers' records of service, The National Archives of the United Kingdom, London. The RFC and the Royal Navy Air Service were consolidated into the RAF April 1, 1918. http://www.forceaerienne .forces.gc.ca/16wing/heritage/hist1_e.asp

visit during the summer: Fallon Tapes, 10–11.

"transferred to the infantry": Fallon Tapes, 12.

"knight of old": Fallon Tapes, 12.

training pilots in Texas: Gayle Pallesen, "John D.: World Was Monopoly Board," *Palm Beach Post-Times,* January 7, 1978.

"lot of fun": JDM to Nixon Smiley, August 14, 1970, Smiley Papers.

CHAPTER 6—EVERY LITTLE BREEZE

44 *Ingalls:* Sometimes misspelled as Ingals, even in court papers. All of Louise's University of Wisconsin papers, including her (or her mother's) original application, use Ingalls, as does Louise's obituary.

varsity: Admissions Recommendation, University of Wisconsin, September 16, 1916; University of Wisconsin yearbook, *The Badger* (1920, for the year 1919), 266, 269, 300; (1921, for the year 1920), 265; grade transcript, Archives, Office of Registrar, University of Wisconsin-Madison.

45 *factory parking lots:* "John D. MacArthur of Bankers Life and Casualty—Building His Own Empire, Lessons of Leadership, Part CX," *Nation's Business,* July 1974, 54.

Carol Frink: Dictionary of American Biography, Supplement 6 (1980), 400–401.

first wife died: Who Was Who in America, vol. iv, 1961–1968, 596; Georgiana Hansen and Edward MacArthur, interview with John Taylor, RG013/SE001/SS001, archives, MacArthur Foundation.

"goiter belt" . . . iodized salt: "Historical Evidence of Benefits of Iodized Salt in the United States," available at http://www.saltinstitute.org/idd.html; http://www.nlm.nih.gov/medlineplus/ency/article/000383.htm.

46 *"disappeared, that's all":* Jean MacArthur Looby, interview with John Taylor, 3, RG013/SE001/SS001, archives, MacArthur Foundation.

Telfer remarried: Ibid., 2.

sons sent him: Richard Harvey, interview with John Taylor, 2, file-Interviews by John Taylor, box #1, Graymont Papers.

"struggled through" . . . "a beard" . . . "certainly not cordial": The first two remarks are from William MacArthur's travel letters, circa April 19 and June 2, 1925, during his visit to China, and the latter comment was recorded during his visit to India, according to a later printing of his letters by Evangelical Printing Co. of Chicago, 21–24; box #2, Graymont Papers.

47 *River Forest: Oak Park Directory and Yearbook,* 1925.

never moved back together: JDM interview with Kiki Levathes, "MacMaestro of the Money Game," *New York Daily News,* July 11, 1976. Louise's obituary listed 1930 as the year of their separation (*Chicago Sun-Times,* March 21, 1979).

CHAPTER 7—CATHERINE T

50 *caught John's eye:* Catherine's birth date is November 23, 1908, on her death certificate, though her 1981 obituaries said she "had turned seventy-two three weeks ago," which would make her birth year 1909 (Gayle Pallesen, *Palm Beach Post*, December 17, 1981).

early 1927: C. MacArthur v. J. MacArthur et al, Complaint, May 6, 1949, Chancery 49C 5461, Circuit Court, Cook County, 2.

her first job: Patricia Hyland, interview with John Taylor, 2, file-Patricia Hyland Interviews, box #1, Graymont Papers.

Navy Pier: Edward MacArthur, Alexander MacArthur, Georgiana Hansen, interview with John Taylor, October 8, 1987, RG013/SE001/SS001, archives, MacArthur Foundation; Patricia Hyland, interview with John Taylor, Graymont Papers.

three boys: Most details on the Hyland family are from Patricia Hyland's memos to or interview with John Taylor, Graymont Papers.

tutors for his children: Edward MacArthur interview with John Taylor; Patricia Hyland interview with John Taylor.

51 *Saint Térèse:* "Saint Térèse of Lisieux," http://womenshistory.about.com/od/teresel/.

"made it alone": Patricia Hyland to John Taylor, memo, 2.

laundry truck . . . gas station: C. MacArthur v. J. MacArthur et al, Complaint, May 6, 1949, 2.

"so and so": Edward MacArthur, interview with John Taylor, 13.

52 *were cheating:* Alexander MacArthur, interview with John Taylor, 36.

"for you": Fallon Tapes, (45).

"end of my career": Ibid., (46).

both were working: C. MacArthur v. J. MacArthur et al, Complaint, May 6, 1949, 2.

"handful as it goes by": Ben Stein, "Everybody's Business," *New York Times*, October 15, 2006.

53 *"make it easy for you":* "John D. MacArthur of Bankers Life and Casualty," *Nation's Business*, July 1974, 54.

script done earlier: Arthur Dorlag and John Irvine, *The Stage Works of Charles MacArthur*, 7.

54 *Nyack: Nyack in the 20th Century*, 79, 118; Hecht, "Charles MacArthur, a Eulogy," 23, box -John D. MacArthur/MacArthur Foundation, archives, Historical Society of Palm Beach County, Palm Beach, FL; William MacAdams, *Ben Hecht*, 109.

"to be villains": Dorlag and Irvine, *The Stage Works of Charles MacArthur,* 5.

"were peanuts": Helen Hayes with Sandford Dody, *On Reflection,* 141–144; Ben Hecht, *Charlie,* 103; Jhan Robbins, *Front Page Marriage,* 38, 175, though this version of the story has Charlie mailing the emeralds to Helen from India with the "peanuts" line on an accompanying card.

55 *roil the waters:* Robbins, *Front Page Marriage,* 81.

"of all meaning": Hayes, *On Reflection,* 160.

lobster diable: Hecht, *Charlie,* 142. Wedding details also from *New York Times,* August 18, 1928; Robbins, *Front Page Marriage,* 80–82.

"remain mated": Hecht, *Charlie,* 82. Later, Carol filed a $100,000 alienation-of-affection suit in Chicago, but withdrew the charges three days into the high-profile trial (Robbins, *Front Page Marriage,* 130–132).

1942: John MacArthur v. Louise MacArthur, Divorce Decree, March 22, 1942, City Court, Calumet City, IL.

1930: Obituary, Louise Ingalls MacArthur, *Chicago Sun-Times,* March 21, 1979.

"struck by her youth": Fallon Tapes, 21.

Drexel . . . Monarch . . . Marquette: Report of Examination of Marquette Life Insurance Company for September 30, 1930, 2, archives, Illinois Division of Insurance.

56 *assets of $15: C. MacArthur v. J. MacArthur et al,* Complaint, May 6, 1949, 3. Regarding the Marquette Life Insurance Co. purchase, there is some confusion in dates and financial data between Catherine's statement in the 1949 Complaint, the state Insurance Examination of September 30, 1930, and the first major local or national article about John in *Fortune,* July 1958 (where the information presumably came from John). I am relying primarily on the first two sources, though in some ways the chronology in the usually reliable *Fortune* makes more sense.

$54.89: Report of Examination, Marquette Life, September 30, 1930, 3.

140 South Dearborn: Report of Examination, Marquette Life, September 30, 1930, 2. Records cannot be located to document whether John was already in control of the company when the name was changed to Marquette, June 10, 1929. He certainly was in control on March 24, 1930, when the Insurance Division approved the relocation of the principal office to 140 S. Dearborn.

Chicago Landmark: City of Chicago Department of Planning and Development, Landmarks Division, http://www.ci.chi.il.us/Landmarks/M/Marquette.html. The building is now owned by the MacArthur Foundation, which has its headquarters offices on the upper floors.

CHAPTER 8—STAYING AFLOAT

58 *"toughest"*: JDM obituary, *Chicago Daily News*, January 6, 1978, quoting earlier interviews.

"handsprings for hamburgers": Fallon Tapes, 23.

$10.28: Report of Examination of Marquette Life Insurance Company, September 30, 1931, archives, Illinois Division of Insurance.

Hoover's . . . campaign . . . Central Life Insurance: Obituaries, *Chicago Tribune*, Alfred MacArthur, December 14, 1967, and Telfer MacArthur, January 30, 1960.

of course, refused: T. A. Wise, "The Incorrigible John MacArthur," *Fortune*, July 1958.

59 *"economic society"*: Professor Joseph M. Belth, "A Brief History of *The Insurance Forum*," http://www.theinsuranceforum.com/history.html.

base their rates: Professor Irving Pfeffer, *World Book Encyclopedia* (1972 ed.) vol. 10, 242.

big boys: on the basis of net retentions, Best's Life Insurance Reports, 1931, Legal Reserve Life Insurance Companies, 1474–1481.

wastebasket: Senator Bob Graham, interview with author; John R. (Rick) MacArthur, "Commentary—A Man Too Decent to Be Nominated," *Providence Journal*, April 6, 2004. Rick MacArthur, not a fan of his grandfather's, adds in his column, "Whether or not he actually threw claims away (Bankers *was* notoriously slow in paying them), he loved to shock respectable people. . . ." JDM was not always clear about which company's "early days" he was talking about in these stories.

"instant dismissal": Katherine Kaluso, interview with author.

61 *and John sued him:* Erwin McKendry, interview with author.

$712.05: Wise, *Fortune*, July 1958, 209. An official Report of Examination of Marquette Life for 1933 could not be found in the Illinois Insurance Division archives.

CHAPTER 9—THE MOTHER LODE

64 *"swindle the people"*: "John D. MacArthur of Bankers Life and Casualty," *Nation's Business*, July 1974, 55.

$631.11: Report of Examination, Bankers Life and Casualty, December 31, 1934, 8, and cover letter June 4, 1935, 1, archives, Illinois Division of Insurance.

$2,500: Report of Examination, Bankers Life and Casualty October 31, 1935, 7, archives, Illinois Division of Insurance.

following day: Ibid., 2.

now belonged to John: Ibid.; also T. A. Wise, "The Incorrigible John MacArthur," *Fortune*, July 1958, 209, and many subsequent press interviews with JDM about the acquisition of Bankers Life and Casualty. This was the name of the company when JDM took control. If someone had deliberately chosen a name similar to the better-known and respected Bankers Life of Des Moines, it was not MacArthur, as some critics would charge. (Report of Examination of Bankers Life and Casualty July 31, 1933, and December 31, 1934; James T. Griffin to William Kirby, memorandum of August 8, 1988, file-William T. Kirby, box #1, Graymont Papers.)

65 *Marquette office . . . assistant treasurer:* Report of Examination of Bankers Life and Casualty, October 31, 1935, 1, 3.

"wife readjust": Fallon Tapes, (43).

cash in hand: Katherine Kaluso, interview with author.

"broke all rules": Fallon Tapes, (42).

66 *$70,000 in the bank:* "John D. MacArthur of Bankers Life and Casualty," *Nation's Business,* July 1974, 56; Wise, "The Incorrigible John MacArthur," *Fortune,* July 1958, 209.

$20 million . . . $166,000: C. MacArthur v. J. MacArthur et al, Complaint, May 6, 1949, Chancery 49C 5461, Circuit Court of Cook County, 5.

terra-cotta: Report of Examination, Bankers Life and Casualty, August 31, 1946, 23.

67 *"rain forest":* All employees have colorful tales about the Bankers' building complex.

half-painted for years: Katherine Kaluso, interview with author.

maneuver: Milan Huba, interview with author. Several folders in the archives of Illinois Insurance Division document the mergers: BL&C—Reinsurance, Illinois Standard Life; BL&C—Reinsurance, West Side Assessment Life; BL&C—Merger, Hotel Men's Mutual Benefit Assoc.; and a separate folder, Hotel Men's Mutual Benefit Assoc.

Illinois Standard Life Insurance: "Bankers Life and Casualty—Reinsurance Illinois Standard Life Insurance," folder in the archives, Illinois Insurance Division.

"mutual assessment association": The history section, 9, of the exceptionally detailed Report of Examination, December 31, 1977 (shortly before JDM's January 1978 death), and subsequent report of February 25, 1980, defined Bankers as originally "an assessment legal reserve life insurance company," Illinois Standard as "a stock legal reserve life insurance company," and Hotel Men's as a "mutual assessment association."

surviving corporation: Certificate of Merger, archives, Illinois Division of Insurance.

68 *"goodwill":* Resolution of Board of Directors of Bankers Life and Casualty, February 8, 1943.

sole stockholder: Insurance regulations required that a small percent of stock be held by directors, as "qualifying shares." In 1970, at the time the John D. MacArthur

Trust No. 1 was established, John held all but eight of five million shares of Bankers Life (Report of Examination, February 25, 1980, 4).

ledger book: Hotel Men's ledger, Bankers Life archives. The "1879" written at the top of the first page is in pencil and was probably added later. Sometimes the date of incorporation is used: April 6, 1880 (Report of Examination of Bankers Life, February 25, 1980, 9).

$1,200: Report of Examination, June 17, 1912, as quoted in documents on the Hotel Men's Mutual Benefit Association of U.S. and Canada, Bankers Life archives.

Chicago's First Insurance Company—Established 1879: Special series of 1948 ads, reprinted in the 125th Anniversary Calendar, Bankers Life, 2004.

69 *"big organization":* Stewart Alsop, "America's New Big Rich," *Saturday Evening Post,* July 1958, 44.

"idea will work": Ibid.

70 *on the city:* Ben Hecht, *Charlie,* 210.

"glamorous suit": Ibid., 211.

served in France: "J. Roderick MacArthur Is Dead," *New York Times,* December 16, 1984.

Okinawa: Edward MacArthur, interview with John Taylor, 21, RG013/SE001/SS001, archives, MacArthur Foundation.

"It's a Great Life": *Theatre Arts News Service,* vol. 1, no. 9 (1954).

broken leg: Georgiana MacArthur Hansen, interview with John Taylor, 21, archives, MacArthur Foundation.

"speaking to anybody": Jean MacArthur Tooby, interview with John Taylor, 2, file-Interview with Grandchildren, box #1, Graymont Papers.

71 *family decided:* Edward MacArthur, interview with John Taylor, 14–15.

friends and relatives: Edward MacArthur, interview with John Taylor, 24.

Hotel Astor: *Time,* August 5, 1940, "People" section.

72 *fingers burned after awhile:* Sandy (Edward) MacArthur, conversation with author, and with John Taylor, 15.

CHAPTER 10—DIVORCE . . . AND DEATH

74 *early in 1948: J. MacArthur v. C. MacArthur,* Complaint for Divorce, April 21, 1949, 49S 5556, Superior Court of Cook County, 2.

"mind of her own": Patricia Hyland, interview with John Taylor, 9, file-Patricia Hyland Interview, box #1, Graymont Papers.

too close: Katherine Kaluso, interview with author.

eventually . . . cleared: Wise, "The Incorrigible John MacArthur," *Fortune*, July 1958, 210.

better than anyone: C. MacArthur v. J. MacArthur et al, Complaint, May 6, 1949, Chancery 49C 5461, Circuit Court of Cook County, 6.

75 *soltero—single:* J. MacArthur v. C. MacArthur, Answer of Defendant, April 22, 1949, 49S 5556, Superior Court of Cook County, 2, 19, (Exhibit D, 2), 25 (Exhibit E, 2), (6) (Exhibit A,1).

charging desertion: J. MacArthur v. C. MacArthur, Complaint for Divorce, 2, April 21, 1949, 2.

pointed out: J. MacArthur v. C. MacArthur, Answer of Defendant, Superior Court, Chancery 49S 5556, 2.

fly right: C. MacArthur v. J. MacArthur et al, Complaint, May 6, 1949, 16–24.

76 *App-Fee Account:* Ibid., 19–20.

"Employees' Welfare Account": Ibid., 20.

their differences couldn't be reconciled: Wise, "The Incorrigible John MacArthur," *Fortune*, July 1958, 212.

settlement: "Dismiss Suit in M'Arthur Business Rift," *Chicago Tribune*, June 23, 1949.

divorce action . . . dismissed: J. MacArthur v. C. MacArthur, Order, September 28, 1949, 49S 5556, Superior Court.

77 *"good friends":* Pat Hyland, interview with John Taylor, 9, file-Patricia Hyland Interview, box #1, Graymont Papers.

"wonderful": Kiki Levanthes, "MacMaestro of the Money Game," *New York Daily News*, July 11, 1976.

"convenience, I guess": Fallon Tapes, 25.

Attu: Edward MacArthur, interview with John Taylor, 25, RG013/SE001/SS001, archives, MacArthur Foundation.

78 *"make it go":* "Brother Act," *Time*, January 3, 1949, 42.

"his friends": John MacArthur, Foreword, in Dorlag and Irvine, *The Stage Works of Charles MacArthur*, x.

Haig and Haig: Helen Hayes, *On Reflection*, 163.

denial: Ben Hecht, *Charlie*, 217–222; Fallon Tapes, 25.

"losing a leg": Hecht, *Charlie*, 217

79 *rang in his head:* Ibid., 128.

"wanted to drink": Fallon Tapes, 25.

Mrs. MacArthur: Betty Perry, interview with author.

final years: Fallon Tapes, 36.

died shortly thereafter: Hayes, *On Reflection,* 226.

poliovirus: Daly Walker, MD, interview with author.

80 *grieving parents:* Fallon Tapes, 26.

"as much beauty as could die": Hecht, *Charlie,* 217. The poet's lines are from "Epitaph on Elizabeth, L.H.," written in 1616.

visited more regularly . . . burial arrangements: John Taylor, interview with retirement home staff, file-Christ's Home, box #1, Graymont Papers.

William's funeral: Edward MacArthur, interview with John Taylor, 5, 14; Pennsylvania death certificate, William T. MacArthur, November 12, 1949, file-Vital Records, box # 2, Graymont Papers. Galt, where William MacArthur is buried, later became part of the city of Cambridge, Ontario.

81 *"good grandfathers":* Judith Krom to Jay Mapstone, January 31, 1989, box #2, Graymont Papers.

"irreverence and bitterness": Thomas Bailey to Rexford A. Boda, Mapstone, Graymont, and Taylor, box #2, Graymont Papers.

internal hemorrhage: obituary, *New York Times,* April 22, 1956.

eulogy . . . in Manhattan: Ben Hecht, "Charles MacArthur: A Eulogy," 1956, Historical Society of Palm Beach County.

82 *"sliding down a banister":* Hecht, *Charlie,* 160–161; also included as an essay under the name "Let's Make the Hero a MacArthur," in *The Grove Book of Hollywood,* Christopher Silvester, ed.

"do no wrong": Dorlag and Irvine, *The Stage Works of Charles MacArthur,* Foreword, John D. MacArthur, ix.

money in MacArthur/Hecht productions: Fallon Tapes, 35.

83 *contemporary Brooklyn:* Mark Fearnow, *Clare Boothe Luce,* 4, 16–19, 130, 186.

shut down the production: Fallon Tapes, 34.

basic problem: Ibid.

Blackfriars: Fearnow, *Clare Boothe Luce,* 134–135.

"unsuccessful politician": Duncan Groner, "Meet John D. MacArthur, America's Least Known Billionaire," UPI, March 19,1972.

with General MacArthur: William Manchester, *American Caesar,* 683–686; Geoffrey Perret, *Old Soldiers Never Die,* 575–577; D. Clayton James, *The Years of MacArthur: Triumph & Disaster 1945–1964,* 648–652.

84 *"different today":* Groner, "Meet John D. MacArthur," UPI, March 19, 1972. A Florida writer, Duncan Groner had originally written a profile on JDM for the

October 1971 issue of *Florida Trend.* Recognizing a good storyteller when he interviewed one, Groner tried to get John to let him write his biography. Such a book was "premature," responded John. "I am sorry, but my answer is a firm 'no.'" (JDM to Duncan Groner, September 14, 1971, Smiley Papers.)

late 1940s: Alex MacArthur, interview with John Taylor, 34. RG013/SE001/SS001, archives, MacArthur Foundation.

"too ancient to be traced": Graymont/Taylor, *The MacArthur Heritage*, 96.

CHAPTER 11—HAT TRICK

86 *special hearing . . . "virtually unscathed":* T. A. Wise, "The Incorrigible John MacArthur," *Fortune* (July 1958), 212. In November 2006, the transcript and the final report of the October 1951 hearing could not be located by the Illinois Division of Insurance in its archives, nor could the Bankers Life regular examination for the following year (1952) be found. *Fortune* reported that MacArthur successfully got substantial court-ordered changes in the 1952 triennial report.

260,000 Georgia policyholders: AP (Atlanta), *Chicago Tribune*, January 30, 1952.

87 *"ridiculous":* AP (Atlanta), *Chicago Tribune*, July 22, 1951.

employees' welfare fund: AP (Atlanta), *Chicago Tribune*, January 30, 1952.

legislative act: AP (Atlanta), *Chicago Tribune*, February 23, 1952.

couldn't make it . . . Mammy's Shanty . . . cigarette package: Derick Daniels, "Vows $500 Paid Her for Cravey Files," *Atlanta Constitution*, March 17, 1953.

88 *left the restaurant:* Georgia Court of Appeals, *Ross v. The State*, June 20, 1952, available at http://vlex.com/vid/20498806. Also *Chicago Tribune*, June 21, 1952 and March 20, 1953; *Atlanta Constitution*, March 17 and 20, 1953; *Fortune*, July 1958, 212–214. Interestingly, only the *Fortune* interview with MacArthur mentions the role of the hat.

$30 million in damages: Chicago Tribune, April 26, 1952.

evidence of the bribe: Atlanta Constitution, March 25 and 27, 1953.

against Cravey: Atlanta Constitution, July 3, 1954.

89 *"premium receipts":* "My Day," December 4, 1953.

handicapped workers in Chicago: Wise, *Fortune*, July 1958, 129.

not to trip . . . how to sign: Kert Brown, interview with author.

over their shoulders: Scott Mikkelsen, informal recollections of employees, archives of Bankers Life and Casualty.

more than a third of . . . employees: Look, February 10, 1953, 19.

"be fired": Stewart Alsop, "America's New Big Rich," *Saturday Evening Post*, July 17, 1965, 26.

90 *Greek cross in 1934:* Blue Cross Blue Shield Association, http://www.bcbs.com/about/history/birth-of-the-brands.html.

Iowa in 1950: AP (Des Moines), *Council Bluffs Nonpareil,* March 9, 1950.

drop the fight: Wise, *Fortune,* July 1958, 212.

along the bottom: For instance, see *Reader's Digest,* February 1972 issue.

"White Cross men": "Living History—Bankers Celebrates 125 Years," *Bankers Life,* vol. 5, issue 4, 2004 (6).

cuff links . . . cigarette lighters: Items in Bankers Life and Casualty archives; "Living History—Bankers Celebrates 125 Years," *Bankers Life,* vol. 5, issue 4 (2004), 15.

91 *"grim realities of actuarial tables":* "Insurance: Putting a Premium on Sales," *Incentive Marketing,* February 1980, 25.

full-time effort . . . $30,000 Life in one month: Bankers Life, June 1952, 10.

Edgewater Beach Hotel: Bankers Life, July 1952, 21–22. Years later in 2004, the company's 125th Anniversary Calendar included (for October) a photograph of a Bankervett dinner dance from 1951.

92 *watch the baby:* Details on working for Bankers Life are based on author interviews with past and present employees.

once a year: C. MacArthur v. J. MacArthur et al, Complaint, May 6, 1949, Chancery 49C 5461, Circuit Court of Cook County, 20.

El or the bus: 125th Anniversary Calendar (December).

just checking: Ibid. (April).

93 *"not in itself a nuisance": Chicago Tribune,* July 18, 1954.

Illinois . . . four more states: Report of Examination of Bankers Life and Casualty, December 31, 1943, 4, and August 31, 1946, 4, archives, Illinois Division of Insurance.

fourteen states: Wise, *Fortune,* July 1958, 212.

$100 million in premium income: Chicago Tribune, March 15, 1954.

navigational aid: "Neighborhood landmark 'Retired,'" *Life at Bankers,* June 1984. The rest of the tower was removed in 1984.

CHAPTER 12—DOWN AMONG THE SHELTERING PALMS

94 *major hurricanes: South Florida Sun Sentinel,* http://www.sun-sentinel.com/news/weather/hurricane/sfl-hc-canehistory1,0,3352010.special.

"bad repair": Palm Beach Post, May 18, 1955.

had foreclosed: : Palm Beach Post, May 15, 2005; *Grants and Deeds, Palm Beach County Florida,* deeds vol. 1076, 634–648; vol. 1049, 201; vol. 1063, 356; vol. 1077, 126; vol. 1113, 624.

97 *"rises and falls"* . . . *"wilderness"*: James Michener notes, typescript [1978], local
history room, North Palm Beach Public Library; pamphlet "The North Palm
Beach Country Club"; *Grants and Deeds*, vol. 1076, 648.

Conch fishermen: David R. Thompson and Sandra Thompson, *Palm Beach from the
Other Side of the Lake*, 23; Michener typescript.

coconut palm trees: Planning document n.d., North Palm Beach Public Library. Northern Dade County was trimmed again with the creation of Broward County in 1915.

population . . . Palm Beach County: U.S. Census Bureau, http://www2.census.gov/
prod2/decennial/documents/41983291.pdf. Population for Palm Beach County
in 2004 was estimated at more than 1.2 million.

98 *"make a living here"*: "Defining Palm Beach Gardens Is Easy," *Palm Beach Garden
Times*, October, 13, 1999.

"entire areas": Bill McGoun, *Palm Beach Post*, November 4, 1984.

another foreclosure: Palm Beach Life, January 1969, 67.

Carol City stock: T. A. Wise, "The Incorrigible John MacArthur," *Fortune*, July
1958, 218.

"just be one more": Ibid.

"stop libeling me": Nixon Smiley, "A Man Involved in Money," *Miami Herald Sunday
Magazine*, November 7, 1965; *Palm Beach Post*, "MacArthur, 'Luck and the PGA,'"
February 24, 1971.

nice earrings: Catherine MacArthur to Nixon Smiley, October 15, 1965; Smiley to
CM, October 25, 1965, Smiley Papers; Smiley, *Miami Herald Sunday Magazine*,
November 7, 1965.

99 *"their needs were met"*: Joel Philips, interview with John Taylor, file-Interviews by
John Taylor, box #1, Graymont Papers.

100 *"think I am?"*: John R. (Rick) MacArthur, *Providence Journal*, April 6, 2004; Bob
Graham interview with Rick MacArthur, 2004, transcript; Bob Graham interview with author, 2006.

$25 an acre: Sarasota Journal, January 4, 1978.

whole new village: Author James Michener, a resident of the village of North Palm
Beach, claimed that MacArthur was erroneously given credit for developing
North Palm Beach. Though MacArthur owned the land, contractors named Ross
actually developed the village, according to Michener's typed 1978 notes in the
village history archives of the North Palm Beach Public Library. The Ross brothers, according to Michener, "went about business sensibly, quietly and modestly."
MacArthur, on the other hand, "loved the public life with its flamboyance."

model home: Palm Beach Life, January 1969, 67.

comfortable circumstances: Stewart Alsop, "America's New Big Rich," *Saturday Evening Post,* July 17, 1965.

101 *"wouldn't have gone through with it":* Palm Beach Life, January 1969.

cover was blown: Richard Austin Smith, "The Fifty-Million-Dollar Man," *Fortune,* November 1957.

"furor": Chicago Tribune, October 29, 1957.

102 *"in color"* . . . *"reporter knocked"* . . . *"other nine":* "A Mogul Steps Down," *Miami Herald,* April 15, 1973.

"demimonde": Wise, "The Incorrigible John MacArthur," *Fortune,* July 1958, 129. Rod MacArthur, a sometime commercial photographer, took at least two of the photos for the 1958 article.

Parmesan: Ibid., 212.

"admit . . . prove": Ibid., 128.

CHAPTER 13—BANYAN TREES AND HIBISCUS HEDGES

104 *"couldn't afford me":* Paul Doolen, typed notes about JDM, n.d., 1, file-Paul Doolen, box #1, Graymont Papers.

spectacular growth . . . *"every phase of company":* Ibid.

old Ford truck . . . *in cash:* Paul Doolen interview with John Taylor, file-Paul Doolen, box #1, Graymont Papers.

105 *1955 . . . what you should have done:* Arlington Heights Herald, January 7, 1978.

friends . . . Bankers' attention: Paul Doolen interview with John Taylor; William Kirby, "My Start with John D. MacArthur," 1987 draft, 1–2, file-William Kirby, box #1, Graymont Papers.

"would make a good man": The receipt had been carefully preserved as a MacArthur artifact by Paul Doolen, box #1, folder and envelope "Paul Doolen Materials," Graymont Papers.

106 *no pirate:* Patricia S. Barberio, *Palm Beach Gardens,* pamphlet (1976), 4.

swampy: Palm Beach Post, July 3, 1970.

manatees: Barberio, 12; *(North Palm Beach County) WeekDay,* June 27, 1979.

a little rain: Barberio, 5; *Sunshine Service News,* October 1962, 25; *Life,* April 1, 1961.

two barges: Sunshine Service News, October 1962, 25; Florida State Archives, print collection, PR 12573.

107 *RCA:* The Palm Beach Gardens RCA plant converted to semiconductor manufacturing and then closed in 1986; Rob Kleppinger, "Early Transistor History at RCA,"

oral history, available at http://www.semiconductormuseum.com/Transistors/
RCA/OralHistories/Kleppinger/Kleppinger_Page3.htm.

reduce RCA's insurance rates: Barberio, 6.

Horatio Alger awards: Chicago Tribune, May 14, 1961.

fastest-growing city: Ibid.

new turnpike: "John D. MacArthur of Bankers Life and Casualty," *Nation's Business,*
July 1974, 53.

108 *commuted from Chicago: Palm Beach Post,* July 3, 1970.

refused to issue the bonds: Barberio, 10; Paul Doolen obituary, *Palm Beach Post,* December 10, 1990.

sewage treatment: Barberio, 10.

couldn't keep up: Barberio, 6.

"monument": (North Palm Beach County) WeekDay, June 27, 1979.

"anything else": Stewart Alsop, "America's New Big Rich," *Saturday Evening Post,*
July 17, 1965, 46.

CHAPTER 14—HOGS GET SLAUGHTERED

110 *only if Feil stuck around:* Marty Bernstein, interview with author; *New York Times,*
May 24, 1962, 48.

111 *do-it-yourself lawyer kit:* William Kirby, "My Start with John D. MacArthur," December 1987 draft, 8, file-William Kirby, box #1, Graymont Papers.

"it was his money": Bernstein, interview with author.

sometimes got twitchy: Dan Childs, interview with author.

if he could swim: Jerome Kelly interview with John Taylor, 1, file-Interview by John
Taylor, box #1, Graymont Papers.

"hogs get slaughtered": Ibid., 3.

flamboyant and shrewd: William Zeckendorf with Edward McCreary, *Zeckendorf,* 262.

112 *"to get out":* Jon Nordheimer, "Florida's Accessible Billionaire," *New York Times,*
June 3, 1973.

"leverage": Zeckendorf, *Zeckendorf,* 6.

collapse: Ibid., 3–4; *New York Times,* obituary, October 2, 1976.

"paid me" . . . "Big Bill": Nixon Smiley, typescript, miscellaneous notes, n.d., Smiley
Papers.

feasibility study: Bob Burdick, "How Disney World Almost Came to Palm Beach
County," *Palm Beach Post-Times,* April 28, 1974, interview with JDM. Jerry Kelly

put the figure that MacArthur, Disney, and RCA contributed at $250,000 each (Kelly to John Taylor, 2).

113 *switch . . . to NBC:* Ibid. Earlier, Walt Disney had tried a similar deal to get financing for California's Disneyland, using a proposed Disney television show to leverage Disneyland funding from NBC and CBS, but both said no. Upstart ABC finally agreed to the deal, which also gave the network, among other things, partial ownership of, and ten-year income from, the amusement park's food concessions. Disney eventually switched to NBC in 1961. (Marc Eliot, *Walt Disney: Hollywood's Dark Prince*, 221–222, 250.)

slipped quietly . . . bit it off: Joel Engelhardt, "How Old Man MacArthur Bullied, Bulldozed, and Built Northern Palm Beach County," *Palm Beach Post*, May 15, 2005.

270 acres: Bob Thomas, *Building a Company: Roy O. Disney and the Creation of an Entertainment Empire*, 187.

"neon jungle": Ibid., 277.

"in the nose": Engelhardt, *Palm Beach Post*, May 15, 2005. *Post* editorial writer Joel Engelhardt's excellent and extensive look at JDM's impact on Palm Beach County was published fifty years after MacArthur's arrival and several months before the death of Jerry Kelly.

114 *"natural death":* Burdick, *Palm Beach Post-Times*, April 28, 1974. West Palm Beach officials later tried another pitch to Disney for a different site; it too was turned down. MacArthur's only involvement was to give them a Disney contact.

World's Fair: Thomas, *Building a Company: Roy O. Disney and the Creation of an Entertainment Empire*, 251–252.

Gentle Ben: Joel Engelhardt, "This Land Ready for Prime Time," *Palm Beach Post*, February 17, 2004, available at http://palmbeachpost.com/.

spread himself too thin: Nixon Smiley, "Impossible? MacArthur Ignored Advice," *Miami Herald*, March 1, 1968.

"too lazy to write": Jone Johnson Lewis, "Your Guide to Women's History," available at http://womenshistory.about.com.

115 *$1.5 million . . . $40,000:* Sheila Tryk, "MacArthur, 'Luck' and the PGA," *Palm Beach Post*, February 24, 1971.

CHAPTER 15—THE COLONNADES

118 *dredged inlet:* "Palm Beach Shores, Past and Present," booklet, rev. ed. 1998, 2, 5; Town of Palm Beach Shores website, www.townhall.ci.palm-beach-shores.fl.us.

heir to the Singer sewing machine fortune: "Singer Island History," http://www.singerisland.com/history.html.

Singer died: "Mr. Paris Singer, Sudden Death in a London Hotel," June 30, 1932, http://www.torbytes.co.uk/.

119 *Blue Heron . . . "Singer's Island":* "Palm Beach Shores," 1998, 3.

A. O. Edwards: "Palm Beach Shores," 1998, 3; typescript n.d., local history room, North Palm Beach Public Library.

"modest means" . . . FHA: Full-page ad from *Miami Herald,* February 19, 1950, Town of Palm Beach Shores website.

"warm in winter": Sales brochure, "Palm Beach Shores, Past and Present," [c.1950], Town of Palm Beach Shores website.

wrong image: Typescript, North Palm Beach Public Library.

$650,000: JDM to Paul Doolen, January 10, 1967, file-Paul Doolen, box #1, Graymont Papers. The letter, detailing the many mortgage, tax, and bond problems JDM was having with the Colonnades' financing during remodeling showed that even MacArthur could run short of cash on occasion. When it closed ten years after MacArthur's death, the Colonnades, though by then decrepit, was valued at $25 million.

"ten-foot pole": Nixon Smiley, "Viewing Florida," *Miami Herald,* August 29, 1965.

120 *"something distinctive":* Nixon Smiley, "The Last Billionaire," 308, typescript of unpublished manuscript, Smiley Papers. This is a chapter Smiley apparently wrote about MacArthur for his 1983 book, *On the Beat and Offbeat,* but it wasn't included in the published version of the book.

little remaining: Smiley, *Miami Herald,* March 1, 1968.

"kitchen and hide": *New York Times,* June 3, 1973.

"Fide et Opera": Brochure, n.d., Historical Society of Palm Beach County. The Latin is also sometimes translated as simply "faith and work." A similar version of the crest and motto was on the cover of printed copies of Ben Hecht's eulogy for Charles MacArthur.

121 *Roney Plaza: Miami Herald,* February 1, 1979.

according to local legend: Photo in private collection of Dan Childs; *Palm Beach Post,* February 12, 1990; and *Palm Beach Daily News,* October 18, 1973.

surprised Hope: "John D. MacArthur of Bankers Life and Casualty," *Nation's Business,* July 1974, 57.

"spectacular": Palm Beach Post, February 12, 1990.

MacArthur's Frontier Hotel: George Stamos, in "The Great Resorts of Las Vegas," *Las Vegas Sun Magazine,* April 8, 1979, writes that Bankers Life exercised a purchase option in early 1965 and that Frontier Operating Company (with thirty-five stockholders) took over the lease from MacArthur and

Bankers Life two years later; Tom Sommer, archives, University of Nevada Las Vegas.

122 *buying spree:* Richard Hack, *Hughes: The Private Diaries, Memos and Letters,* 291.

"and I left": Smiley, "The Last Billionaire," unpublished manuscript, Smiley Papers. JDM told a magazine reporter for *Nation's Business* in 1974 that he "never talked personally with him [Hughes]" during the Frontier transaction.

"Treasure Isle": http://www.classicthemes.com/50sTVThemes/themePages/treasureIsle.html.

Amaryllis: Stephen Pounds, "The End of the Colonnades," *Palm Beach Post,* February 12, 1990.

123 *seminar for state legislators:* Bob Graham, interview with author.

bipartisan group: Alan Rosenthal, interview with author.

124 *"money, sex, health, crime":* "The Sensuous Publisher," *Forbes,* June 15, 1971.

lived for a month: "The published books of William Hoffman," http://writer-services.com/home/Book_List.asp (accessed July 10, 2006).

Bankers Life company publications: Elliott Bernstein, "The Misanthrope as Billionaire," *Business Week,* August 1, 1970, 6.

"more an act of spite": Ibid.

"historical fact": Graymont/Taylor, *The MacArthur Heritage,* 98.

John himself: Edward MacArthur, interview with John Taylor; Billie MacArthur (Mrs. Edward MacArthur), interview with author. Hoffman was a prolific writer, and many of his later books would, in fact, be ghostwritten autobiographies, in addition to his biographies of Paul Mellon and David Rockefeller (which critics claimed borrowed heavily from a *New Yorker* profile).

"lies" . . . "money from it": Bob Sanford, *John D. MacArthur: A View from the Bar,* 80.

125 *"hurt his feelings":* John Irvine, interview with author.

"downplayed the luck": Sheila Tryk, *Palm Beach Post-Times,* November 7, 1971.

"worse it stinks": Memo from JDM to Paul Doolen, August 28, 1974, file-Paul Doolen, box #1, Graymont Papers.

"well-sharpened blade": Clarus Backes, "An Incomplete Hatchet Job," *Chicago Tribune,* January 13, 1970.

CHAPTER 16—FOUNDING A FOUNDATION

128 *cow manure:* Phil Catasus Jr., son of pilot Felipe Catasus, interview with author.

tracheotomy: William Kirby, "The Formation of the John D. and Catherine T. MacArthur Foundation," typescript, draft December 1987, 5, file-William Kirby, box #1, Graymont Papers. Graymont writes (96, note 23, presumably reviewed by Kirby) that this document was a draft for a speech.

stomach cancer: Jon Nordheimer, "Florida's Accessible Billionaire," *New York Times,* June 3, 1973; Kiki Levathes, "MacMaestro of the Money Game," *New York Daily News,* July 11, 1976.

129 *"Sugar":* Dan Childs, interview with author; Tom Burke, "The Sweeter Options of John D. MacArthur and Truman Capote," *Esquire,* December 1970, 258.

Harney Pond Canal: Buck Island Ranch History, Archbold Biological Station Website, http://www.archbold-station.org.

160-acre grove: Archbold Biological Station Newsletter, Fall 1991, 4.

130 *black-crested caracara:* Margery Gordon, "A Natural Alliance," *New Times Broward-Palm Beach,* March 25, 1999, http://www.newtimesbpb.com/issues/1999-03-25/feature.html.

south of Vero Beach . . . "participating partner" . . . "good buy": Childs, interview with author; *Hereford Journal,* July 1986, 213; Childs, memoir/Anita Childs obituary, handwritten manuscript; Childs, "Buck Island Ranch," memoir/general ranch information, handwritten manuscript.

131 *never leave the house:* Catasus, Jr., interview with author.

large central room: Childs, interview with author; author's visit to ranch.

"if he's honest": Gerald Storch, "He's Not Your Average 'Mr. Rich,'" *Miami Herald,* March 6, 1976.

132 *long screened porch:* Kirby, "Formation of the John D. and Catherine T. MacArthur Foundation," 9.

"earn an honest dollar": Childs, interview with author.

"better salesman than you are": Kirby, "Formation," 2.

tell over and over: Richard Kaplan, MacArthur Foundation, interview with author. Kaplan says Bill Kirby consistently told the same version of the story of the foundation's origins.

133 *"people you trust":* Kirby, "Formation," 8, 9.

"any charitable purpose": Kiki Levanthes, "MacMaestro of the Money Game," *New York Daily News,* July 11, 1976.

134 *"helped build it up":* This story, and other details of signing, are from Kirby, "Formation," 12–15.

kitchen table: Ibid., 16.

"what I do best": Ibid., 11.

"qualified charitable organizations": Ibid., 11–12.

CHAPTER 17—PALM BEACH PROMETHEUS

136 *light breeze . . . twice :* Lincoln Werden, "Nicklaus Wins PGA Crown Second Time," *New York Times,* March 1, 1971.

MacArthur neighbor: In early 2007, Jack Nicklaus dedicated a refurbished and re-designed municipal golf course as a gift to the North Palm Beach community; it was near, if not part of, the same land whose "rises and falls" had once caught the fancy of Sir Harry Oakes (see Chapter 12, James Michener notes); "North Palm Beach Country Club Celebrates Grand Opening," available at http://www.nicklaus.com/design/npbcc/011907.php.

sumptuous PGA clubhouse: Sheila Tryk, "Why the World Cup? MacArthur Wanted It Here," *Palm Beach Post-Times,* November 7, 1971.

Pinehurst, North Carolina: Palm Beach Post, April 11, 1971, quoting March 21 issue of the *Chicago Tribune.*

137 *"save the PGA": New York Times,* November 3, 1972.

"run the bases": Michael Walsh, "PBG Honors Founder with MacArthur," *Palm Beach Times,* July 5, 1972.

"debacle": Robert Sobel, *RCA,* 10–11.

ocean frontage: Palm Beach Times, June 23, 1970.

fallen in love: Miami Herald, August 7, 1977.

the Alba: Access: Miami and South Florida (New York: HarperCollins, 1999), 164.

floodlights: Ibid.

ten-week season: "Palm Beach History," Worth Avenue Association, available at http://www.worth-avenue.com/palm_beach_story.

138 *health problems: Palm Beach Times,* June 23, 1970.

"to the bottom": Nelson Manfred Blake, *Land Into Water—Water Into Land,* 298.

139 *endangered lands:* Ibid., 227–229. Blake names as the key bills the Water Resources Act of 1972, Environmental Land and Water Management Act of 1972 (ELMS), State Comprehensive Planning Act, and Land Conservation Act; see also Bill McGoun, *Palm Beach Post,* November 4, 1984.

cap on . . . living units: McGoun, *Palm Beach Post,* November 4, 1984.

humility: Blake, *Land Into Water,* 301.

"permit from somebody": JDM quoted by Norv Roggen in the *Palm Beach Post,* April 6, 1973.

throwback: Ann Burton, North Palm Beach Public Library, conversation with author.

"still around": Roggen, *Palm Beach Post,* April 6, 1973.

"Florida passport": Georgia Martinez, "A Mogul Steps Down," *Miami Herald*, April 15, 1973.

CHAPTER 18—LOST AND SOMETIMES FOUND

142 *on hand:* Bankers Life newsletter, March 1972, 13.

university level: Richard Fallon, interview with author.

"leading playwrights": "President's Remarks," Senate Resolution No. 1138, Florida State Archives, Tallahassee, FL.

143 *"more than he has ever given me"*: Helen Hayes to Duncan G. Groner, as quoted in Groner's UPI story "Meet John D. MacArthur, America's Least Known Billionaire," March 19, 1972.

papers around the country: For instance, the *Los Angeles Times*, March 19, 1972.

delighted: John Irvine, interview with author; Richard Fallon, interview with author.

144 *private sources: Florida State Reports*, (a publication for FSU alumni and parents), March 1974.

operating expenses . . . covered mainly by John: Florida State University cultural affairs director Alan Sapp, as quoted in *Palm Beach Times*, August 31, 1978.

writing talent: Fallon, interview with author.

"American theatre": Dorlag and Irvine, *The Stage Works of Charles MacArthur,* vii.

145 *"theatrical world with him"*: Both Richard Fallon and John Irvine told the author that neither had ghostwritten John's essay, and that as far as they knew JDM wrote it himself.

preserving material about Charlie: Nixon Smiley to Mrs. John MacArthur, November 5, 1965, Smiley Papers.

making the trip . . . womanizer: Fallon, interview with author.

146 *"want a jury trial" . . . supporting roles:* Ibid.

"rude to you": Helen Hayes with Sandford Dody, *On Reflection*, 178.

147 *"memory is better"*: Norv Roggen, *Palm Beach Post*, April 6, 1973.

gone now: The exact death dates for the MacArthur siblings are: Alfred, December 13, 1967; Telfer, January 29, 1960; and Helen Bishop, December 15, 1974.

Rick, born in 1956: Born shortly after Charles MacArthur's death, the baby was given the full name of John Roderick Charles Gordon MacArthur. Therefore, the John R. MacArthur who is today listed on the masthead of *Harper's Magazine* is not a junior, even though the full name of his father, Rod, was John Roderick MacArthur.

visit the ranch: Rick MacArthur, interview with author.

at least a higher salary: Joel Phillips, interview with John Taylor, RG013/SE001/ SS001, archives, MacArthur Foundation.

"about a car?": Rick MacArthur, interview with author.

148 *troubled marriage:* Joel Engelhardt, *Palm Beach Post*, May 5, 2005.

Rome newspaper: Paul Hofmann, "Kidnappers Free Getty, 17, in Italy," *New York Times*, December 16, 1973.

robbed and murdered: Richard T. Griffin, "The Feuding MacArthurs," *New York Times*, January 23, 1977. When Griffin asked about the event, John shrugged off the question and, according to the article, couldn't remember his grandson's name, saying, "I have so many grandchildren." (He had seven, counting the missing Greg.) But then MacArthur had suffered a stroke just two months before the phone interview.

"twenty-six years old": *Chicago Sun-Times*, January 8, 1978.

"somebody" in Washington: Roberta O'Brien, interview with John Taylor, RG013,SE001/SS001, archives, MacArthur Foundation.

149 *real party:* Phil Lewis, interview with author.

"rich man": Ibid.

CHAPTER 19—ROYAL SUMMONS

152 *"have it framed":* *Palm Beach Post*, July 6, 1976.

invitation list: Guest list, 7/7/76, folder John D. MacArthur, box 1970, White House Central Files Name File, Gerald R. Ford Library, Ann Arbor, MI.

153 *in a taxi:* Richard Fallon, interview with author.

round of golf: Jerry Ford to JDM, July 16, 1976, folder John D. MacArthur, box 1970, White House Central Files Name File, Ford Library; Gayle Pallesen, "Mac-Arthur: An Era Has Ended," *Palm Beach Post-Times*, January 7, 1978.

Bankers Life on occasion: Paul Doolen, memo to John Taylor, file-Paul Doolen, box #1, Graymont Papers; Kiki Levanthes, "MacMaestro of the Money Game," *New York Daily News*, July 11, 1976.

White House grounds: State dinner details from *New York Times*, July 7 and July 8, 1976.

154 *"not accepting it":* Billy Graham, *Just As I Am*, 471–472.

"turned and walked away": Excerpt from After-Dinner Remarks of Dr. Billy Graham, Friday evening, prior to dedication of the Graham Center, Wheaton, IL, September 15, 1980, Graymont Papers. Graham said this occasion was the last time he ever saw MacArthur.

"The Lady Is a Tramp": Helen Thomas, "At 90, Ford Still His Old Charming Self," http://www.thebostonchannel.com/helenthomas/2356067/detail.html. A photo

of the president and the queen dancing is at the Ford Presidential Library, Ann Arbor, MI, http://www.potus.com/grford/queen.html.

"her squat": Sheri Bergbom, *Palm Beach Post,* July 14, 1976.

"above the average mortal": Lois Wilson, "The Listening Post—Unimpressed by John D.," *Palm Beach Post-Times,* July 18, 1976.

155 *"grateful to you":* JDM to Dr. Richard Brannon, 7/15/76, folder John D. MacArthur, box 1970, White House Central Files Name File, Ford Library.

"here as my witness": Fallon, interview with author.

Bahamas: Fallon, interview with author; Bob Sanford, *John D. MacArthur: A View from the Bar,* 99.

156 *harder than it looked:* Edwin Darby, *The Fortune Builders,* 129.

nailed down in writing: Richard T. Griffin, "The Feuding MacArthurs," *New York Times,* January 23, 1977.

"Current Quotations": "The History of the Bradford Exchange" http://www .thebradfordgroup.com; Holly Miller, "Collectors Bullish on Plates," *Saturday Evening Post,* July/August 1982, 30.

157 *"Great Crockery Raid":* Rod, interview with Edwin Darby, *The Fortune Builders,* 130. Other details from Rod's interview with Griffin, "The Feuding MacArthurs," *New York Times,* January 23, 1977.

fight between accountants: Griffin, "The Feuding MacArthurs," *New York Times,* January 23, 1977.

$1.5 million: Leonard Wiener, *Chicago Tribune,* March 15, 1976.

$35 million: Miami Herald, March 18, 1979.

158 *"D. K." Ludwig . . . uncommunicative:* Jerry Shields, *The Invisible Billionaire: Daniel Ludwig,* 6, 359.

"philanthropist": The Accessible Billionaire, transcript of 1976 audiotape, file-TV CBS Interview with J. D. MacArthur, box #1, Graymont Papers.

"into one thing": Phil Robertson, *WeekDay,* July 14–20 1976.

159 *"all along":* Ibid.

"get started": Karen Schickedanz, "Work, Pride in It Spell Happiness for Bankers Life Chief," *Chicago Tribune,* March 11, 1973.

"get a license": The Accessible Billionaire, TV interview, 1976.

"breaking your way": Schickedanz, *Chicago Tribune,* March 11, 1973.

$7 million: Marty Bernstein, interview with author; Carol Oppenheim, "Billionaire MacArthur: A Contented Man," *Chicago Tribune,* March 15, 1976; Kiki Levanthes, "MacMaestro of the Money Game," *New York Daily News,* July 11, 1976.

"greatest mother": Palm Beach Post-Times, November 13, 1976.

"choked on an ice cube": "MacArthur's Stroke Confirmed," *Palm Beach Post*, December 24, 1976.

160 *"for a rest"*: *Chicago Tribune*, December 5, 1976.

insisted . . . "unintelligible": *Palm Beach Post*, December 24, 1976.

frustrating: Nixon Smiley, "The Last Billionaire," 321, unpublished typescript, Smiley Papers.

CHAPTER 20—AND WITH DIGNITY

162 *pecan pie*: Gayle Pallesen, interview with author; Pallesen, *Palm Beach Post*, March 14, 1977, and *The Washington Post*, March 15, 1977.

163 *"in the back"*: Ray Mariotti, *Austin (Texas) American-Statesman*, January 8, 1978.

MacArthur himself had started: Bankers Life company publication, 1973.

"JDM in March": Bankers Life company publication, 1973, "JDM and the Spirit of '76."

vacillated: Pallesen, interview with author.

164 *"dreams turn gray"*: Ibid.; Pallesen, *The Washington Post*, March 15, 1977.

see his cousins: Edward MacArthur, interview with John Taylor, 25, RG013/SE001/SS001, archives, MacArthur Foundation.

The Tontine: Catherine Hyland to Nixon Smiley, Smiley Papers.

detective stories: Pat Hyland interview with John Taylor, 6, file-Patricia Hyland, box #1, Graymont Papers.

straitlaced: Georgiana MacArthur Hansen, interview with John Taylor, 25, RG013/SE001/SS001, archives, MacArthur Foundation.

165 *Lalique crystal*: Pat Hyland, interview with Taylor, 7.

frugality rubbed off on her: Mr. and Mrs. Paul Doolen, interview with John Taylor, 3, file-Paul Doolen, box #1, Graymont Papers.

"artificial chicken": Gayle Pallesen, "World's Greatest Tell the Folks How They Did It," *Palm Beach Post*, June 27, 1977.

166 *"my nurse" . . . medicine*: Pallesen, interview with author.

"vigor": Ibid.; Pallesen, "Painter Neiman Captures Nature and MacArthur," *Palm Beach Post-Times*, June 26, 1977.

ducks: The messy ducks were gone within days of JDM's death, wrote lawyer Bill Kirby ("The Formation of the John D. and Catherine T. MacArthur Foundation," draft, December 1987, 11, file-William T. Kirby, box #1, Graymont Papers).

make the rounds: Pallesen, interview with author.

formerly delighted him: Dan Childs, interview with author.

nation's second-largest . . . Robert Ewing: Martin Baron, *Miami Herald,* January 7, 1978.

field force . . . in forty-seven states: Best's Insurance Reports—Life/Health, 1977, 233–235.

net earnings . . . admitted assets: Ibid.

$1.04 billion: Illinois Department of Insurance, Report of Examination, February 25, 1980, 1. (This examination is for the period of January 1, 1971 through December 31, 1977.)

167 *make a few jokes: Miami Herald,* October 21, 1977; Gayle Pallesen, "MacArthur: An Era Has Ended," *Palm Beach Post-Times,* January 7, 1978.

central and southern Colorado: Complaint, U.S. Federal Trade Commission, docket no. 9075, filed May 28, 1976; Decision and Order, August 27, 1979, 1, 4; Illinois Insurance Examination, February 25, 1980, 6.

largest cash settlement: Seth King, "Buyers to Get Refunds on Worthless Land in Colorado," *New York Times,* May 10, 1979.

Holley by the Sea: UPI wire service *(Miami Herald),* August 23, 1977; Fred E. Fogarty, "Magna . . . A Potent Power in Florida Land," *Fort Lauderdale News and Sun-Sentinel,* March 26, 1978.

"never fooled him": Tim Pallesen, *Miami Herald,* January 4, 1978.

"no misinformation": Gayle Pallesen, *Palm Beach Post,* January 4, 1978.

"and with dignity" . . . "recover his health": JDM to Paul Doolen, August 2, 1972, file-Paul Doolen, box #1, Graymont Papers.

168 *recognize her: Palm Beach Times,* January 5, 1978.

"business as usual": Katherine Kaluso, interview with author.

CHAPTER 21—GENIUS

170 *ashes scattered:* James D. Tilford, Jr., to Gayle Pallesen, January 19, 1988.

"departed friends": Charles Mount, "Short Will, with Sense of Humor," *Chicago Tribune,* January 7, 1978.

171 *"sell more insurance":* R. C. Longworth, "Tempo—Two Parties Live in the Wake of John MacArthur's Death," *Chicago Tribune,* March 10, 1979.

"will have to": Ibid.

"would have wanted" . . . "right idea": Gayle Pallesen, "Billionaire Has His Last Wish," *Palm Beach Post,* June 24, 1979.

$2 billion: The Foundation Directory, 1983, as quoted by *Weekly Business,* June 17, 1985.

$5.023 billion . . . ranked eleventh: The Foundation Directory, 2006 Edition. The ten largest foundations ranked by assets (using 2004 fiscal information, unless otherwise noted) are: 1) Gates, 2) Ford, 3) J. Paul Getty Trust (operating), 4) Robert Wood Johnson, 5) Lilly Endowment, 6) W. K. Kellogg (2005 data), 7) William and Flora Hewlett, 8) David and Lucile Packard, 9) Andrew W. Mellon, and 10) Gordon and Betty Moore.

first two grants: "MacArthur at 25: Confronting Challenges, Making a Difference," April 19, 2004, http://www.macfdn.org/anniv/ (accessed April 19, 2004).

172 *conflicts of interest . . . knew and trusted:* Bob Tamarkin, "Bitter Charity," *Forbes,* June 11, 1979, 113–114.

$60 million: James T. Griffin, memorandum to William Kirby, August 8, 1988, file-William T. Kirby, box #1, Graymont Papers.

no success: Richard Fallon, interview with author.

dropped from payroll: Joe Bizzaro, "MacArthur's FSU Theater Plan Faces Crisis," *Palm Beach Times,* August 31, 1978; Fallon, interview with author.

partially dispersed: Vic Meyrich, Asolo Theatre, Sarasota, FL, interview with author. After the collection was shipped (apparently in poor condition) from Florida State University to the Asolo, material concerning the historic Yiddish theater and Actors Studio later was taken for the Belknap Collection for the Performing Arts at the University of Florida, Gainesville. Meyrich, disturbed at seeing the collection broken up, eventually drove some fifty cartons back to Tallahassee, where they were stored in a warehouse. There, following inquiries from this book's author, student researcher Mary Gunderlach, working under the direction of Professor Lynn Hogan of the FSU School of Theatre, located the long-missing tapes and transcripts of Richard Fallon's interviews with John MacArthur.

173 *legal place of residency:* "Florida Set to Do Battle on MacArthur Estate Tax," *St. Petersburg Times,* January 11, 1978; "Illinois, Florida in Battle Over Tycoon's Estate Tax," *Chicago Tribune,* January 11, 1978.

where he voted: Chicago Tribune, January 11, 1978.

"Tax from Billionaire's Estate Low": South Florida Sun-Sentinel, November 16, 1978.

wildlife habitat: http://www.archbold-station.org; author visits to Archbold Biological Station and to MacArthur Agro-ecology Research Center/Buck Island Ranch, Lake Placid, FL.

"weeds in the canal": Dan Childs, interview with author.

ignored his father, Rod: Rick MacArthur, "The Real Hero of Air Force Beach," *Palm Beach Post,* August 9, 1997.

"give it to the folks": William Kirby, "My Start with John D. MacArthur," draft, December 1987, file-William Kirby, box #1, Graymont Papers; Gayle Pallesen, "MacArthur's Legacy," *Palm Beach Life,* January 1991.

174 *"fashionably left-wing"*: http://www.discoverthenetwork.org; Dore Carroll, "The Iconoclast Upstairs: *Harper's* Rick MacArthur," *The New York Review of Magazines*, 2001, available at http://www.jrn.columbia.edu.

"from the grave": Carol Oppenheim, "Billionaire MacArthur: A Contented Man," *Chicago Tribune*, March 15, 1976.

175 *"sympathetic chord"*: Marcia Pounds, "MacArthur Legacy Lives," *Weekly Business*, June 17, 1985, 3.

"persistence . . . conceptual obstacles": Fellows Program Overview, Frequently Asked Questions, the MacArthur Foundation website, http://www.macfound.org.

editorial . . . Burch: The editorial was "Of Venture Research," *American Heart Journal*, December 1976, according to the MacArthur Foundation website. Dr. George Burch, whose papers are at the National Institute of Health (http://www.nlm.nih.gov/hmd/manuscripts/ead/burch.html) died in 1977, before seeing the launch of the MacArthur Fellows Program.

"pressure to publish": Fellows Program Overview, Frequently Asked Questions, MacArthur Foundation website, http://www.macfound.org; Denise Shekerjian, *Uncommon Genius: How Great Ideas Are Born*, xiv.

"needed to be free": "A Fund for Genius," *Newsweek*, August 13, 1979.

176 *lived . . . modestly:* Art Petaque and Hugh Hough, "Late Billionaire's Daughter Forced to Live Modest Life in Mexico," *Chicago Sun-Times, Houston Chronicle*, March 11, 1979.

exceeded $25 million: Patricia Hyland, memorandum, n.d., to John Taylor, box #1, file- Patricia Hyland Interview, box #1, Graymont Papers.

Conseco . . . colorful officers: Bill W. Hornaday, "Conseco Files for Bankruptcy," *Indianapolis Star*, December 18, 2002; Greg Andrews, "Hilbert: Successors' Performance 'Turns My Stomach'," *Indianapolis Business Journal*, October 9–15, 2006; Charles V. Bagli, "Poof! $34 Million Vanishes on Broadway," *New York Times*, September 26, 1999.

177 *"waste our money on nonsense"*: JDM to Paul Doolen, August 28, 1974, file-Paul Doolen, box #1, Graymont Papers.

SELECTED BIBLIOGRAPHY

Antel, Francis P. *Ransom and Gems: The DeLong Ruby Story*. Palm Beach: Literary Investment Guild, 1969.

Barberio, Patricia S. *Palm Beach Gardens*. Pamphlet. [Palm Beach Gardens Bicentennial Committee, 1976.]

Best's Insurance Reports, Life-Health. Various vols. Oldwick, NJ: A.M. Best Co.

Blake, Nelson Manfred. *Land into Water—Water into Land: A History of Water Management in Florida*. Tallahassee: University Presses of Florida, 1980.

Boorstin, Daniel J. *The Discoverers*. New York: Random House, 1983.

Cannon, James M. *Time and Chance: Gerald Ford's Appointment with History*. New York: Harper Collins, 1994.

Carroll, Bob. *The Importance of Pancho Villa*. San Diego: Lucent Books, 1996.

Chernow, Ron. *Titan: The Life of John D. Rockefeller, Sr.* New York: Random House, 1998.

Costain, Thomas. *The Tontine*. Garden City, NY: Doubleday & Co., 1955.

Curl, Donald W. "The Early Days." In *Palm Beach County: In a Class by Itself*. Fort Lauderdale, FL: Copperfield Publications, 1998

Darby, Edwin. *The Fortune Builders*. Garden City, NY: Doubleday & Co., 1986.

Dorlag, Arthur, and John Irvine, eds. *The Stage Works of Charles MacArthur*. Tallahassee: Florida State University Foundation, with the Charles MacArthur Center and the School of Theatre, Florida State University, 1974.

Eliot, Marc. *Walt Disney: Hollywood's Dark Prince*. Secaucus, NJ: Carol Publishing Group, 1993.

Fearnow, Mark. *Clare Boothe Luce: A Research and Production Sourcebook*. Westport, CT: Greenwood Press, 1995.

Fleishman, Joel L. *The Foundation—A Great American Secret: How Private Wealth is Changing the World.* New York: Public Affairs, 2007.

The Foundation Directory. Various editions. New York: The Foundation Center.

Graham, Billy. *Just as I Am: The Autobiography of Billy Graham.* San Francisco: Harper San Francisco/Zondervan, 1997.

Graymont, Barbara, author, and John Taylor, project director and interviewer. *The MacArthur Heritage: The Story of an American Family.* Chicago: John D. and Catherine T. MacArthur Foundation, 1993.

Guarino, Jean. *Yesterday: A Historical View of Oak Park, Illinois.* Vol. 1, *Prairie Days to World War I.* Oak Park, IL: Oak Ridge Press, 2000.

Hack, Richard. *Hughes: The Private Diaries, Memos and Letters.* Beverly Hills: New Millennium Press, 2001.

Hayes, Helen with Sandford Dody, *On Reflection: An Autobiography.* New York: M. Evans and Co., 1968

Hayes, Helen with Lewis Funke. *A Gift of Joy.* New York: M. Evans and Co., 1965.

Hecht, Ben. *Charlie: The Improbable Life and Times of Charles MacArthur.* New York: Harper and Brothers, 1957.

Hellman, Geoffrey. *Bankers, Bones and Beetles.* Garden City, NY: Natural History Press, 1969.

Historical Society of the Nyacks. *Nyack in the 20th Century.* Pearl River, NY: Star Press, 2000.

Hoffman, William. *The Stockholder.* New York: Lyle Stewart, 1969.

Holbrook, Stewart H. *The Age of the Moguls.* Garden City, NY: Doubleday, 1953.

James, D. Clayton. *The Years of MacArthur: Triumph and Disaster 1945–1964.* Boston: Houghton Mifflin, 1985. [Gen. Douglas MacArthur]

Johnston, Hank. *Death Valley Scotty: The Man and the Myth.* Yosemite, CA: Flying Spur Press, 1972.

MacAdams, William. *Ben Hecht: The Man Behind the Legend.* New York: Scribner, 1990.

Manchester, William. *American Caesar: Douglas MacArthur, 1880–1964.* Boston: Little, Brown and Co., 1978.

Nasaw, David. *Andrew Carnegie.* New York: Penguin Press, 2006.

Nielsen, Waldemar A. *The Big Foundations.* New York: Columbia University Press, 1972.

——— *The Golden Donors.* New York: E. P. Dutton, 1985.

The Nyacks and Piermont. Various vols. Newburg, NY: Breed Publishing Co.; *Richmond's Directory of Nyack.* Yonkers, NY: W. L. Richmond, 1914–1915.

Old Nyack: An Illustrated Historical Sketch of Nyack-on-the-Hudson. Nyack, NY: Nyack National Bank, 1928.

Robbins, Jhan. *Front Page Marriage*. New York: G.P. Putnam's Sons, 1982.

Perret, Geoffrey. *Old Soldiers Never Die: The Life of Douglas MacArthur*. New York: Random House, 1996.

Preston, Douglas J. *Dinosaurs in the Attic*. New York: St. Martin's Press, 1986.

Sanford, Bob. *John D. MacArthur: A View From the Bar—A Memoir*. Highland City, FL: Rainbow Books, Inc., 1996.

Schulte, Gary. *The Fall of First Executive: The House That Fred Carr Built*. New York: HarperBusiness, 1991.

Shekerjian, Denise. *Uncommon Genius*. New York: Viking-Penguin, 1990.

Shields, Jerry. *The Invisible Billionaire: Daniel Ludwig*. Boston: Houghton Mifflin, 1986.

Silvester, Christopher. *The Grove Book of Hollywood*. New York: Grove Press, 2000.

Smiley, Nixon. *On the Beat and Offbeat*. Miami: Banyan Books, 1983.

Sobel, Robert. *RCA*. New York: Stein and Day, 1986.

Strouse, Jean. *Morgan: American Financier*. New York: Random House, 1999.

Thomas, Bob. *Building a Company: Roy O. Disney and the Creation of an Entertainment Empire*. New York: Hyperion, 1998.

Thompson, David Robinson and Sandra Thompson. *Palm Beach: From the Other Side of the Lake*. New York: Vantage Press, 1992.

Wallace, Joseph. *A Gathering of Wonders*. New York: St. Martin's Press, 2000.

Whitney, Courtney. *MacArthur: His Rendezvous with History*. New York: Alfred A. Knopf, 1956. [Gen. Douglas MacArthur]

Zeckendorf, William with Edward McCreary. *The Autobiography of William Zeckendorf*. New York: Holt, Rinehart and Winston, 1970.

INDEX